SPOTLESS

SPOTLESS

Room-by-room solutions to domestic disasters

Shannon Lush & Jennifer Fleming

EBURY
PRESS

1 3 5 7 9 10 8 6 4 2

First published in 2005 by ABC Books for the AUSTRALIAN
BROADCASTING CORPORATION

This edition published in 2008 by Ebury Press, an imprint of Ebury
Publishing

A Random House Group Company

The Random House Group Limited Reg. No. 954009

Addresses for companies within the Random House Group can be found at
www.randomhouse.co.uk

A CIP catalogue record for this book is available from the British Library

The Random House Group Limited supports The Forest Stewardship Council (FSC), the
leading international forest certification organisation. All our titles that are printed on
Greenpeace approved FSC certified paper carry the FSC logo. Our paper procurement policy
can be found at www.rbooks.co.uk/environment

To buy books by your favourite authors and register for offers visit www.rbooks.co.uk

Printed and bound by CPI Mackays, Chatham ME5 8TD

ISBN 9780091922566

Designed by Nanette Backhouse /saso content & design

CONTENTS

ACKNOWLEDGEMENTS

Thanks to all the women in my family, especially Mum, for fabulous training. Thanks to my beautiful daughters, Erin and Tamara, for being there for me. Thanks to my wonderful and helpful husband Rick, who puts up with a workaholic wife and is incredibly supportive of everything that I do. I'd also like to thank James Valentine, Richard Fidler, Carole Whitelock, Bernadette Young, Alison Buchanan, Louise Saunders and Pam O'Brien for their continuous support and encouragement. And most especially Jennifer Fleming, the wonderful writer, who turned a dream into a reality.

Shannon

This book would not have happened without James Valentine, who reinvented handy hints talkback on his Afternoon Show on 702 ABC Sydney. Thanks, James, for your encouragement of this project through all its stages. Thanks to Stephen Amery from 702 ABC Sydney for kindly copying old radio programmes for me. Photographer Steven Godbee produced beautiful and stylish images and my big thanks go to him. Thanks to Susan Morris-Yates and the team at ABC Books. My parents, Pat and John Fleming, read early drafts and gave their advice. Tony Speede distracted me when required. And big thanks to Shannon Lush for her incredible knowledge. I've learned so much!

Jennifer

Introduction

Have you ever accidentally put a jumper in the washing machine and found it will now only fit a twelve-year-old? I have. Do you know what to do if you burn a pan, aside from chucking it out? I do. What do you do if your lovable pooch has a mishap on your white wool carpet? I know.

The good news is that there are solutions to these and many other problems that occur in and around the home, and this book will show you how to fix them. It also offers guidance on the correct way to do all those things you're not really quite sure how to do. Things like how to vacuum properly, how to organise your wardrobe, and the best way to wash dishes.

This book will also give you the confidence to walk past those expensive cleaning products in the supermarket. Because we know less and less about cleaning, advertisers can play on our fears of not being quite clean or hygienic enough. We will buy an overpriced product that promises instant cleaning because we think it could rescue us from becoming a social pariah. Well, there's no need to be seduced any longer. You will learn to love bicarbonate of soda. Vinegar won't just be part of a salad dressing. And here's something you won't hear about in one of those gleaming-white ads on TV: the best cleaners are water and sunshine.

This book is a room-by-room guide to your house. There's information on how to care for and fix just about anything that can go wrong in each room. The advice is set out like a cookbook so you can see which 'ingredients' or cleaning products you'll need before following the 'recipe' or cleaning process. You'll also find real-life questions from people who've called me when I've appeared on the radio. If you have a problem that isn't covered in this book, contact me through my website: www.shannonlush.com.

There are a couple of tricks with stain removal. Firstly, don't panic and put something on the stain that could make it worse. Work out what's in the stain. Then work out what the solvent is. If there are several components to the stain, you must remove the protein part first, then fats, then any chemical or biological dyes, and then any resins or glues. The way to work this out is to remember that proteins are anything animal-or seed-based, fats are greasy between your fingers, and resins and glues are not water-soluble. If you're not sure, clean with cold water first, then use hot water, then any solvents.

You'll read a lot about 'blood-heat water' in the book. This is lukewarm or warm water. The way to test the temperature is to put the water on your wrist; if you can't feel it – if it's not too hot or too cold – it's blood heat.

When using vinegar, you'll get a better result if you use cider vinegar on hard surfaces and white vinegar on fabrics or white marble.

Dry-cleaning fluid is the same thing as white spirits or *Murlex*, which is a brand of dry-cleaning fluid.

When you come across the two-sponge method for bicarb and vinegar, it means that you dip one damp sponge in bicarb and another in vinegar, then lay the vinegar sponge over the top of the bicarb sponge and squeeze the two together as you clean. As an alternative, if you're working with an intricate surface, make a paste of bicarb and water to the consistency of soft butter. Paint it over the surface with a cloth, leave it to dry and then polish off with a rag dipped in vinegar.

And if you're feeling disheartened while cleaning or tackling that stubborn stain that just won't shift, just think about the Exxon Valdez disaster when thousands of litres of oil spilled into an Alaskan harbour. Your disaster will never be as bad!

SHANNON'S STORY

One of my earliest memories is of my grandmother coming over to help Mum clean the house. I would watch as brass and silver were polished and stains were removed. The house would be filled with the smell of beeswax. Even now, when I open a tub of *Gumption*, I'm reminded of my grandma.

My mother trained as a tailor and taught me to sew. She's absolutely brilliant with a needle and sewing machine and is such a great cleaner that the family refers to her as 'the white tornado'. My father was an engineer, artist, builder and inventor and knew a great deal about chemicals. He always explained what something was, why it worked and how chemicals react with each other. I think learning that kind of information at such a young age made it instinctive for me.

As a child, I loved anything creative. I loved using coloured pencils, painting and sewing. At the age of eight, I sold my artwork to school classmates so they could enter art competitions! Sewing classes at primary school were taught by Mrs Roberts, who was from the old school and stiff as a ramrod. Before each class, you had to wash your hands and anyone with sweaty palms had to pat their hands with talcum powder. Everything was done by hand; every seam had to be backed. I learned how to do fairy stitches, embroidery and petit point. At the time, we all thought Mrs Roberts was a dragon but her attention to detail and craft was an invaluable example to me.

I turned these skills into a living when I was a teenager and embroidering denim was popular. I also set up stalls outside rock concerts and painted people's faces. Then I got a job in the rag trade which taught me about the line and hang of fabric. I became a lot faster at sewing and sold things at markets. I learned every craft that

I could: ceramics, glass, leadlighting, painting, sculpture, working with metals and making jewellery.

The move into ceramics opened up a whole new area for me. After winning several awards at competitions, I set up a makeshift shop at the bottom of my sister's house. One day, a woman came in with damaged ceramic and asked if I could repair it. I did some research, managed to fix the piece and the woman was so thrilled she sent her friends along.

This led me into the world of restoration. I spoke with other restorers and studied for some time with a very knowledgeable man who was in his eighties by that time. It was a perfect melding of my artistic skills and my love of antiques and decorative art. When I look at anything antique, I see the tracks of all the hands that have moved over it. And my father's early teaching about chemicals also helped, because restoration often involves breaking something down before rebuilding it.

I've always loved books on handy hints, particularly old ones. My great-aunt Letitia kept a notebook with hints, proverbs, quotations for women, recipes and jokes, which was a wonderful resource. I developed an active interest in stain removal after marking things with paints because, when I'm painting, I make a serious mess. There were plenty of phone calls to my mother for advice. I also test any handy hint I come across. No matter what it is, I'll give it a go.

This book is a collection of that knowledge.

JENNIFER'S STORY

I'm part of the generation that rings Mum for advice on how to fix any spills or stains around the house. And I'm very lucky to have a mum who knows what to do. That's why most of my friends didn't believe me when I told them I was writing a book on household hints. It's not that my house is dirty. They just knew I had very little knowledge in this area. Now, they can't shut me up.

When I was growing up, Mum did show me how to wash up, hang out the washing and iron, but I rarely use those skills today. I take the phrase 'wash and wear' literally. For many years I've paid someone to clean the house, as much for domestic harmony as anything else. All the knowledge in this book is Shannon's. I'm just the absorber and writer of the book.

This book came about through James Valentine and his radio programme on 702 ABC Sydney. He heard the advice that spiders are deterred by lemons, which reminded him of all those old-fashioned handy hints. He asked listeners to ring in if they were having problems fixing a spill or stain around the house and then invited other listeners to give their solutions. One day Shannon rang in and answered every question. She became a regular guest on the programme and has been helping listeners ever since.

I produce James' show and many listeners would ring and ask, 'Does Shannon have a book?' Well, here it is!

USEFUL INGREDIENTS

**0000
steel wool** is a very fine grade steel wool. Available from hardware shops.

Acetone is a volatile, flammable ketone. It's used as a solvent for resins, primers, nail polish and heavy plastics. It's available from chemists and hardware shops.

Beeswax is the wax produced by bees when making honeycomb. It's a great polishing agent.

**Bicarb
(sodium
bicarbonate)** is a salt and an alkaline. It's also known as bicarbonate. Bicarb neutralises acid. During this process it releases carbon dioxide and water which is great for penetrating stains or dissolving grease. It's available at the supermarket, generally in the cake baking rather than cleaning aisle, and at chemists.

Bleach is a whitening agent.

Borax is a crystalline sodium borate. It is a fungicide, insecticide and detergent booster. It is mildly toxic and should be applied with care. Avoid contact with skin and avoid ingesting it. It's available from chemists and some supermarkets.

Camphor is a ketone from the camphor laurel tree. It has a strong vapour which most insects, particularly moths, and cats don't like. It makes a great protector of gardens and wardrobes. It's very flammable so never heat it.

Carpet cleaner   comes in many varieties. They can be soap-based, bicarb-based, detergent-based or alcohol-based.

Chamois block   a fine-grade cleaning block that is a very absorbent sponge which removes moisture from carpet and other surfaces. Punch make one. There's an Australian product called Slurpex available at www.slurpex.com.au.

Cloves   are a spice. They come from the dried flower bud of the clove tree. Oil can be extracted from them and used to inhibit mould.

Cornflour   is a starch of maize, rice and other grains. It's absorbent and a very fine abrasive.

Creosote   is a liquid, oily wood tar distillation used as a preservative and antiseptic. Available from hardware shops.

Descaler   removes limescale and calcium deposits from kettles, coffee machines, steam irons, shower heads, toilets and sinks. It's available in various forms from the supermarket or hardware shops.

Dry-cleaning fluid   is a mixture of petroleum hydrocarbons. It's a solvent and also known as white spirits.

Epsom salts   are hydrated magnesium sulphate and named because they were found at Epsom in Surrey. They are good as a bath soaker and for unshrinking jumpers and other woollens.

Eucalyptus oil   is an essential oil distilled from the leaves of certain eucalyptus trees. It's a paint stripper, adhesive solvent and also releases vapours. Unlike most oils, it mixes with water. It's available at the supermarket or chemists.

Fuller's Earth   is high calcium clay with a bleaching agent. It's very absorbent. It acts as a wool relaxant and is used to unshrink or shrink woollens. It's available from chemists.

Goanna oil   is an oil made from goanna fat. It's used as a lubricant and liniment. It's available from chemists.

Glycerine   is an odourless, clear liquid. It's used as an agent in cosmetics, toothpaste and shampoos and is soluble in both water and alcohol. Glycerine helps loosen stains. It's available from chemists.

Gumption   is a greyish cleaning paste which has many uses. It's great for cleaning the bath and kitchen sink. It contains a mild bleaching agent and abrasive. It's available from the supermarket.

Hydrogen peroxide   is an oxidising liquid used as an antiseptic and bleaching agent.

Lavender oil   is derived from lavender flowers and has many uses including insect repellent, dog inhibitor or air freshener. Buy it at the supermarket, chemists or health food stores.

Leather dew is a combination of soap and oil and used to treat leather. It's available from shoe repair shops.

Lemon oil comes from the oil in a lemon peel and is used as a furniture polish, spider and insect inhibitor and stain remover.

Methylated spirits is a raw alcohol with menthol. The menthol gives it a strong smell and taste so it isn't mistaken for water. It's a solvent for paints.

Oil of cloves is cold-pressed oil from the dried flower bud of the clove tree. It's useful as a mould inhibitor, insecticide, toothache soother and an ingredient in cooking. It's available from chemists.

Oil of pennyroyal is oil from a small-leafed mint. It's useful in deterring moths and fleas, **but is harmful to pregnant women and shouldn't be used by them or near them or in large quantities**.

Plaster of paris is a white powder made of calcium sulphate. It forms a paste when mixed with water and can be shaped before setting. It's also absorbent and good for removing stains from granite. It's available from art supply shops or hardware shops.

Rotten milk is formed by leaving milk in the sun until it forms into solids. The time taken to rot varies according to the weather and age of the milk. Rotten milk is great for removing inks.

Shellac is a varnish made of a resinous substance secreted through the pores of the carapace of the *Coccus lacca* scale insect. This substance is then dissolved in alcohol or a similar solvent. It's used for making varnish, polish and sealing wax.

Sugar soap is a highly caustic soap. It comes in powder or liquid form. The powder form has a mild abrasive.

Sweet almond oil is the oil from almond nuts. It's useful for cleaning bone and ivory. Available from supermarkets and chemists.

Talcum powder is ground from a soft greenish-grey mineral. It's a super fine abrasive, lubricant and is also very absorbent.

Tea-tree oil is an oil extracted from a tea-tree bush. It's used as an antibacterial and mixes with water.

Turpentine is a volatile oil and resin distilled from trees. It's a solvent for oil-based paints.

Unibond PVA is a PVA wood glue and sealant. It's available from hardware shops.

Vanilla essence is extracted from vanilla beans. It is combined with alcohol and provides fragrance and flavour to food.

Also a deodoriser. Available from supermarkets.

Vinegar   is an acid. It's a preservative, condiment, beverage and for our purposes, cleaner and sanitiser. Cider vinegar is best on hard surfaces and white vinegar is better on fabrics and white marble. It's available from supermarkets.

Wet-and-dry   is a very fine (2000 grade) abrasive paper. Available from paint supply and car accessory shops.

Whiting   is a powder used in cleaning and polishing glass. The powder removes excess oil and putty from leadlight panels. It's available from leadlight shops.

Witch-hazel   is extracted from the bark and leaves of a shrub, *Hamamelis virginiana*: witch-hazel or spotted alder. Used as a soothing and mildly astringent and lotion. Available from supermarkets and chemists.

Woolwash   is a mild soap combined with eucalyptus oil and bicarb soda or detergent. As the name suggests, it's useful in washing woollens. Buy it from the supermarket.

WD-40   stands for Water Displacement, 40th attempt. It's a high-grade penetrating oil and stops corrosion.

Wheat Bran   is the ground husk of wheat or other grain. It's absorbent and a scourer and good for cleaning fabrics and furs.

The Kitchen

The kitchen is the centre of the home. It's the room we gravitate to, particularly when we're hungry. Food is stored here, prepared here, served here and often eaten here. It's where the dirty plates and cutlery return, and where scraps and rubbish are dealt with. It's a zone of constant cleaning but also the space for creative culinary expression. Keep it clean and hygienic because it's never a good idea to poison your guests or the children!

A HOT POT ON LAMINATE: JOHN'S STORY

Incident: 'I'm living in a rental property at the moment that has a very 1970s yellow laminate worktop. And I don't know how, but I managed to put a hot pot on the laminate and it's left a scald mark. I've tried all the usual cleaners and nothing has worked. How can I fix it so I get my deposit back?'

Solution: What to do will depend on how deep the burn is. Either way, warm the laminate first with a cloth that's been run under hot water, then wrung out and placed over the affected area. If it's a shallow burn, put dry-cleaning fluid on a cotton wool ball and rub it over the scald. Then rinse it off with a damp cloth. If the scald is deep, put dry-cleaning fluid onto a cotton wool ball, add a dab of *Gumption* and apply the mixture to the scald. Then rinse it off with a damp cloth. If the burn is really bad, you may have to replace a section of the laminate and you'll need a restorer or other professional to help with this.

OVEN

I can still picture my grandmother cleaning the oven. She used to wrap a tea towel over her face in an attempt to block the fumes created by the cleaning agent, caustic soda. It used to stink the kitchen out for a couple of hours. Methods aren't as drastic now, though I prefer to use bicarb and vinegar to clean the oven rather than proprietary products.

Be careful when cleaning ovens because most are made of enamel and steel. Enamel is essentially very tough glass fired onto a steel base and will scratch if you use abrasives and scourers. If you can, wipe the oven every time you use it and clean it properly every couple of uses. Just make sure it's cool enough that you don't burn yourself! Remove the oven racks, rack supports, element and light cover and sprinkle the surface with bicarb, then splash some vinegar over the top. There will be a fizzing when the two come into contact. Scrub with a sponge or nylon brush as soon as this happens. To clean the sides of the oven, use one damp sponge dipped in bicarb, and another sponge dipped in vinegar. Apply the bicarb sponge first, then place the vinegar sponge over the top of the bicarb sponge and press the vinegar through both sponges. Once you've cleaned, rinse with water. If there are stubborn stains or burns, reapply the bicarb and vinegar several times and use a nylon brush to scrub. In order to see what you're cleaning on the oven roof, place a small mirror on the bottom of the oven.

Clean all the bits you removed with bicarb and vinegar. Let them stand before washing in the sink with detergent and water.

If you inherit a very scratched oven, sand it gently with damp 2000-grade wet-and-dry or have it re-enamelled.

Q: 'I've got a huge scorch mark on the oven glass,' says Natalie. 'Is there anything I can do?'

Problem: Scorch marks on the oven glass.
What to use: Bicarb, vinegar, nylon brush.
How to apply: Sprinkle bicarb onto the scorch mark at about the same thickness as you would sprinkle icing sugar onto the top of a cake. Then splash it with an equal amount of vinegar. While it's fizzing, rub it with a nylon brush, then rinse. You may need to repeat this several times.

GRILL

A grill is really just a small oven and should be cleaned the same
way. For day-to-day cleaning, take the removable parts of the grill
out and wash with detergent and water. Most stains should come
off. For any stubborn stains, use bicarb and vinegar as described for
the oven.

HOB AND SPLASHBACK

I almost burned the house down when I was fourteen. It was just
like that ad on TV when the woman leaves some chips cooking on
the hob while she answers the phone. The pan ignites in flames and
she exclaims, 'Oh my goodness, the chips!' It was a bit like that with
me. I was making chips and answered the door. I was only gone for
about two minutes and in that time the plastic on the extractor fan
was in flames and the wiring in the brick wall was also alight. Never
leave a frying pan cooking!

Wipe the area every time you use it with either bicarb and vinegar
or hot water and detergent. Gas jets should be removed and cleaned
in water and detergent. Don't use a scourer because it will scratch
the surface. Make sure all the jets are clear before putting them back.

Problem:	**Smoke marks on splashback.**
What to use:	**Ash, bicarb, vinegar, cloth.**
How to apply:	Use ash from a cigarette or from the fireplace. You need enough ash to make a thin covering over the smoke mark. Rub the ash over the mark and then clean it off with bicarb and vinegar on a cloth.

Problem: **Scratches on the splashback.**
What to use: **Bicarb, sponge, vinegar, or whiting, cloth.**
How to apply: Put bicarb on a sponge and wipe it over the scratch, then wipe over it with a sponge soaked in vinegar. If this doesn't work, use a chalk product called whiting, which is available at leadlight stores. Sprinkle whiting over the scratch as though you're icing a cake and rub the area with a damp cloth.

Problem: **Candle wax on hob.**
What to use: **Ice cube, flat-bladed knife or plastic/wooden spatula, detergent, cloth or old stockings.**
How to apply: Chill the wax by placing ice on it, then scrape as much of it away as possible with a flat-bladed knife. If you're removing wax from an enamel hob, use a plastic or wooden spatula. Then mix cold water and detergent on a cloth to remove any remaining wax. You must use cold water because hot water will soften the wax, spread it and make it harder to remove. If it's really hard to get off, rub the wax with an old pair of stockings or pantyhose. If you are melting candle wax on the hob, use a double boiler and always heat and stir slowly.

Problem: **Chocolate on the hob.**
What to use: **Hairdryer, wet cloth.**
How to apply: Always use a double boiler if you're cooking chocolate on the hob. Burnt chocolate sets like cement and can only be removed with a hairdryer and wet cloth. Lay the wet cloth over the chocolate. Then hold up one edge of the cloth and apply the hairdryer so that the chocolate melts into the cloth.

I learned this trick when I was training to be a
chocolate chef and had plenty of spillages. It also
turned me off the smell of chocolate for years.

COOKER HOOD AND EXTRACTOR FAN

If you think about all the fumes and particles sucked up by the
cooker hood, it's no wonder it needs to be cleaned. Most modern
cooker hoods have stainless steel filters that can be put in the
dishwasher or scrubbed in the sink with detergent and a nylon
brush. Use bicarb and vinegar if the build-up is really stubborn.
Charcoal filters should be washed backwards—that is, where the
smoke comes out—and need to be replaced from time to time.
Check the manufacturer's instructions. Using the extractor fan is the
best way to minimise stains on cupboards and odours in your house.
The cupboard above the oven always ends up greasy. Store canned
goods here instead of plates or glasses that need to be washed to
get all the grease off. And don't leave boxed goods here because
heat and grease affect cardboard and can penetrate the packaging.

POTS AND PANS

Pots and pans can be made of stainless steel, aluminium, teflon,
enamel, copper, cast iron, tin or glass. The best way to wash them is
with detergent and water. Don't put pots and pans in the dishwasher
if the handle is wooden, plastic or bakelite because it will fade and
crack. Stains will come off more easily if you put a small amount of
water and a drop of vinegar in your pots straight after using them.

If you have cast-iron pots, never put them in the dishwasher
because they will rust. Instead, wash them by hand and dry them in
the oven. Set the oven on its lowest temperature and allow it to
warm, then turn it off and leave the cast-iron pot inside until it dries.

Re-season cast iron with a little olive oil rubbed around the base with a paper towel, then let it heat through on the stove for a couple of minutes before wiping again with the same paper towel.

I have a very strong grip so I'm always breaking the plastic handle on lids. And there's nothing trickier than trying to remove a hot lid without a handle. An easy replacement is a brass or ceramic cupboard doorknob with a screw-and-nut back.

Q: 'I cook everything in my old wok,' says Graeme. 'It's got to the point that if I can't cook something in the wok, I won't eat it! But it's accumulated all this build-up which, despite some concerted scrubbing on my behalf, just won't shift. Is there anything I can do?'

Problem: **Burnt pan.**
What to use: **Bicarb, vinegar, nylon brush.**
How to apply: Sprinkle bicarb into the pan then sprinkle vinegar over it. This will make it fizz. Scrub with a nylon brush while it's fizzing. You may need to repeat this two or three times for bad burns.

Problem: **Egg stains in the pan.**
What to use: **Rubber gloves, eggshell, aluminium foil, vinegar.**
How to apply: Put on rubber gloves. Then place half an eggshell together with a strip of aluminium foil and 240 ml of vinegar into the stained saucepan. Leave for half an hour and the egg stain will wipe off. The reason this works is that the calcium in the eggshell leaves a chalky deposit that absorbs the egg. I learned this from Great-aunt Letitia's wonderful notebook.

Problem: Rust in the pot/pan.
What to use: Potato, bicarb.
How to apply: Cut a potato in half and dip the cut surface in some
bicarb. Rub it over the rust and then rinse the pot
or pan in water. The starch and iodine in the potato
remove the rust. The salt reacts with the starch
and iodine and forms a mild caustic.

Problem: Dent in a pan.
What to use: Wooden spoon, hammer.
How to apply: Place the edge of a wooden spoon on the pointed
side of the dent, then tap a hammer lightly onto the
other edge of the wooden spoon until the dent
smoothes out. If the bottom of the pan has a dent,
place one block inside and another block underneath
the pan, then hammer the blocks and it will smooth
out so you can cook evenly again. This technique
can also be used for teflon pans.

 'I picked up some old bakelite canisters at a
second-hand shop,' says Jane, 'but they've got
some scratches on them. Is there anything to be
done?'

Problem: Scratches in old bakelite canisters/handles.
What to use: Sweet almond oil, paper towel or cotton wool
ball or whiting, glycerine, cloth.
How to apply: Apply a small quantity of sweet almond oil with a
paper towel or cotton wool ball. Then wipe it off. If
you have deep scratches, use whiting and glycerine.
Mix ½ teaspoon of whiting with 2½ tablespoons of

glycerine to the consistency of runny cream. Rub the mixture around and around in circles with a cloth until the scratches have rubbed out, then wipe it off.

Problem:	**A glued pot handle has cracked and come loose.**
What to use:	**Butcher's twine, heat-resistant superglue.**
How to apply:	Strap the handle with butcher's twine then cover the strapped handle with heat-resistant superglue. This forms a seal that is hygienic and non-toxic. It can loosen again if washed repeatedly in a dishwasher or if it's left soaking in boiling water.

APPLIANCES

Whether it's grinding coffee or making bread, there's an appliance for everything! Most appliances can be cleaned with detergent and water either in the sink or with a sponge. Clean them as soon as you can because when food sets it becomes much more difficult to remove. Pull the appliance apart as much as possible but never put electrics in water. If there's staining on plastic surfaces, wipe with glycerine first, then use bicarb and vinegar. To remove rust marks on plastic, use a paste of glycerine and talcum powder.

Kettle

I drink massive amounts of tea every day so I'm very used to cleaning the kettle. For general cleaning on the outside, use bicarb and vinegar. Apply with two sponges, one with bicarb on it, the other with vinegar on it. Start with the bicarb sponge then rub the vinegar sponge over the surface.

Q: 'My stainless-steel electric kettle has a build up of gunk from years of use,' says Cecily. 'What should I do?'

Problem:	**Scaling in the kettle.**
What to use:	**Descaler, or bicarb, vinegar, nylon brush.**
How to apply:	Follow the instructions for the descaler, then rinse out with water. Make sure you clean it out well or your next cup of tea will taste a bit funny. You could also try bicarb and vinegar scrubbed with a nylon brush if the area is accessible, but generally the build-up happens under the element so descaler is the best option.

Espresso/coffee machines

Clean with bicarb and vinegar. Any areas that have contact with coffee should then be rinsed with a salt solution, which also makes the coffee taste better. The areas that come into contact with milk need to be cleaned with cold water first to remove proteins and then cleaned with hot water to remove fats. It's not a good idea to use detergent because it curdles milk and makes the curds stick to the surface, encouraging bacterial growth.

Mixers and blenders

Clean the inside of blenders by adding 2 teaspoons of bicarb and 120 ml of vinegar and then switching the blender on. Make sure you cover the blender first or you'll be cleaning the whole kitchen. Then rinse out with water. I used to make pâté for restaurants, and one time I forgot to put the lid on the blender. It was like a volcano spewing hot liver around the kitchen. I was cleaning it up for weeks afterwards. If you're blending anything hot, place a clean tea towel over the blender before you put the lid on. It protects the plastic in the lid from melting, stretching or shrinking and will lessen mess in the kitchen if the lid takes off because of too much heat inside. If the fit is poor, hold the lid with your hand while blending.

Toaster

Clean the outside of a toaster with bicarb on one sponge and vinegar on another sponge. Wipe with the bicarb sponge first, then the vinegar sponge. For the interior, sprinkle coarse salt in the top of the toaster, cover the slots with your hand and shake it up and down a few times. This cleans it and helps prevent vermin. When you've finished, shake the contents into the bin. Make sure you get all the salt out or it may cause corrosion.

How to get stains off an old thermos

To clean an old stained flask or thermos, put 2 teaspoons of bicarb and 120 ml of vinegar inside. Put the lid on and give it a shake, but not for too long or it will explode. Take the lid off, let it sit for half an hour, top it up with hot water and leave overnight. The next morning, give it a shake and rinse.

Microwave

I love the microwave and it's much easier to clean than the oven. The glass or china turntable can be removed and cleaned in the sink with detergent. Make sure it's dry before you replace it or your rollers will rust. Remove the nylon turning ring and wheels and clean in detergent, then dry them.

For the interior, sprinkle bicarb over first, then add vinegar and wipe with a sponge. For the sides and top, use the two-sponge method: wipe with the bicarb one first, then the vinegar one.

I think it's worthwhile learning how to operate the microwave properly because there is an art to good microwave cooking. All microwaves come with an instruction manual and cookbook. If you don't have one, contact the manufacturer and they'll send you one generally free of charge. Also be aware that microwaves have different power settings so each machine will be different.

Problem:	**Food splattered inside the microwave.**
What to use:	**White vinegar, water, bicarb, large microwave-proof bowl.**
How to apply:	Mix 120 ml of white vinegar, 240 ml of water and 1 tablespoon of bicarb in a large bowl. Put the bowl in the microwave without a lid on and cook on high for a few minutes, allowing the mixture to boil, but not boil over, for around 1 minute. While the microwave is warm and steamy, wipe the interior down with a cloth.

Dishwasher

Dishwashers may have saved many relationships, but they've ruined plenty of crockery, cutlery and glassware. I hate them because dishwashers clean by flinging small particles of soap, food and water at high speed, which virtually sandblasts your plates and cutlery. Bear this in mind when putting things in. Never put fine china, crystal, items with gold edging or good cutlery in the dishwasher. Some of the damage won't be fixable, even by me. For other items, always rinse before putting them in. Heat-sensitive items should sit at the top; saucepans should sit at an angle towards the bottom centre of the dishwasher. And don't overpack the dishwasher because china and glass can break if they bang together. Don't put electrical parts in. And always use a good quality soap and rinse agent that dissolves well.

If your dishwasher has an odour, put bicarb in the detergent compartment and vinegar in the rinse-aid compartment and turn the dishwasher on for an empty run. This will clean the drainpipes at the same time. If the dishwasher really stinks, wipe the rubbers and interiors with vanilla essence. This removes the smell and acts as an antibacterial. If the rubbers become perished, they harbour bacteria. To help prevent perishing, rub the surfaces with dry salt and then vanilla essence.

Refrigerator

I'll never forget the state of my friend's fridge when I helped him move house. It had been switched off for a few weeks and the door had been left closed tightly. When we opened it, mould was all the way to the door and filled every cavity. We ended up hosing it clean in the garden.

Most fridges are easy to look after, especially those with auto-defrost. Clean the fridge once a month with bicarb and vinegar. The best time to clean is just before you do your shopping because it'll be fairly empty. Pull the shelves and compartments out and wash them with bicarb and vinegar. To clean the sides of the fridge, put bicarb on one sponge and vinegar on another and press the vinegar sponge through the bicarb sponge when cleaning.

To cut back on cleaning, put a thin foam rubber sheet in the bottom of the crispers. This stops food getting caught in the ridges and slows the rotting process because air circulates around the food. The foam can be washed as well.

Clean the rubber seal around the fridge door with a tea towel soaked in vinegar and bicarb. Then wrap the tea towel over a plastic knife and clean inside all the little grooves. If you can slide a piece of cardboard between the fridge and the seal, it's time to get a new seal. You can buy seals at most hardware shops either sized to fit your model or by the metre. Put them on yourself with an appropriate adhesive.

The exterior of fridges, including stainless-steel ones, should be cleaned with bicarb and vinegar. Cockroaches are attracted to the warm motor in the fridge so scatter salt underneath. If you use cockroach baits, put one behind the microwave, one on either side of the bottom of the stove and one behind the fridge.

Storing steel wool

I cleaned an old freezer with fine-grade steel wool and acciden-tally left the steel wool inside the freezer. When I discovered it, it didn't have any rust on it. I now store steel wool in a plastic bag in the freezer to prevent rust.

Problem:	**Odour in the fridge.**
What to use:	**Small divided dish, vanilla essence, bicarb.**
How to apply:	Try to locate the source of the smell and remove it. Then fill each side of a small divided dish with vanilla essence on one side and bicarb on the other. Sushi condiment dishes work well for this. Place the dish in the fridge and it will absorb the nasty smells and deodorise the fridge.

Problem:	**Defrosting the freezer more quickly.**
What to use:	**Sugar, rubber gloves, rubber spatula.**
How to apply:	After turning the fridge off, sprinkle sugar over the base of the freezer. This speeds up the defrosting process. Use gloved hands or a rubber spatula to remove the ice. Never use a hairdryer or heater because it could crack the coils. Never use a sharp knife or you could pierce the coils and release the gas.

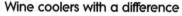

Wine coolers with a difference

An unglazed terracotta tile makes a great cooler. Soak one in water then put it in the freezer ready to use in wine coolers or cool bags. It also helps the ice last longer. Make your own wine cooler with a clean unglazed terracotta flowerpot. Soak it in water and put it in the freezer until you need to use it. The evaporation keeps the wine chilly. Or create a disposable wine cooler from an old wine box bladder. Fill the bladder with water and, with the tap on the outside, wrap it around an empty wine bottle. Then put it in the freezer. It's great for picnics because you'll have iced water on tap when it melts as well as chilled wine.

WORKTOPS

Just as you can age a tree by counting its rings, you can age a kitchen by the kind of worktop it has. If it's mission brown, burnt orange or avocado green it's likely to be from the 1970s. Flecked laminate suggests the 1950s. And stainless steel screams 1990s! No matter the fashion, all of them need cleaning and maintenance. If your kitchen is well ventilated but you have persistent smells, it means you have a build-up on your surfaces or in your plumbing. Wipe the worktop thoroughly each time you prepare food.

Laminate

The best way to keep laminate clean is with bicarb and vinegar applied with sponges. If you get heavy staining with tea or scorch marks, put glycerine on the stain for about 5 minutes then use bicarb and vinegar. Never use abrasives.

Problem: Laminate has come away from chipboard backing or the chipboard is breaking down behind the laminate.

What to use: Water, oil of cloves, *Unibond PVA*, paintbrush, cling film, clamp.

How to apply: Into 60 ml of warm water, mix 1 drop of oil of cloves and stir thoroughly. Then mix 1 tablespoon of this mixture into 1 tablespoon of *Unibond PVA*. Paint this over the chipboard, then wrap the entire join in cling film and clamp it, making sure you have something between the clamp and the bench, such as a magazine or small piece of wood. The mixture will seal the chipboard and the oil of cloves prevents mildew. I learned this after living in some pretty revolting rental properties.

Q: 'I was on a health kick and decided to make beetroot soup,' says Lisa. 'But the lid flew off the blender and beetroot landed all over the laminate worktop. What can I do?'

Problem: Beetroot stains on laminate.

What to use: Vinegar; or glycerine, cotton bud or cotton wool ball.

How to apply: If you are dealing with the stain while it's fresh, clean the area with vinegar. If the stain has set, apply glycerine to the stain with a cotton bud or cotton wool ball; leave for a few minutes then remove. To prevent the problem, put a tea towel over the blender before putting the lid on. If the lid comes off, the tea towel will contain the mess. If the fit is poor, hold the lid on with your hand.

Corian

Corian is a composite of many different materials including quartz, marble, granite, mica, feldspar and synthetics such as polycarbonate, epoxies or cement blends. Clean with bicarb and vinegar. If it has a polyurethane finish, use detergent and water.

Marble

Marble is often regarded as the glamour worktop. But care should be taken when cleaning it because it's porous. The best way to clean marble is by sprinkling bicarb over it and then splashing 1 part vinegar to 4 parts water on top. It's important to dilute the vinegar because full-strength vinegar can react with the lime in the marble and create holes or a rough surface. If the surface isn't sealed with polyurethane or other sealant, use a good quality, liquid hard wax for marble flooring to make it less porous and less likely to absorb stains. The way to tell if marble is covered in polyurethane is to put your eye level with the marble and shine a light along the surface. If the light shines in one uninterrupted beam, it's sealed with polyurethane. If the beam of light has lines and dots, it's unsealed.

Problem:	**Stain in the marble.**
What to use:	**Bicarb, vinegar, water, cling film; or glycerine, cotton wool ball; or salt, lemon.**
How to apply:	To remove fat and oil stains, mix 1 dessertspoon of bicarb, 1 dessertspoon of vinegar and 4 dessert-spoons of water into a light paste. Place the paste on the stain then put cling film over the top of it for no more than 15 minutes. Then remove the mix. The stain should come out as well. For fruit stains, first apply glycerine with a cotton wool ball then use the

above method. For rust stains, place a small
mountain of salt over the stain then squeeze enough
lemon juice to wet the salt. Scrub and repeat. Do not
use descaler on marble because it will dissolve it.

Problem:	**White, chalky-looking chips in the marble.**
What to use:	**Candle wax, hairdryer, soft cloth, marble floor wax.**
How to apply:	Match the candle colour to the marble. Place a small piece of wax over the chip, then use a hairdryer to slightly melt the wax into the marble. Buff it with a soft cloth until it's the same height as the rest of the worktop. Then use a marble floor wax to treat the whole area.

Granite

The best way to clean granite is with bicarb and vinegar. If it has a
polyurethane finish, keep the surface clean because it can bubble.
If you do get bubbles, mix 1 part *Unibond PVA* to 20 parts water and
inject with a syringe. Do this with each bubble and then place a flat
weight over them. A heavy book should do the job but make sure
you have cling film underneath the book so that it doesn't stick.
Check the drying time of the glue on its packet. When it's dried,
wipe off the excess with warm water.

Problem:	**Grease stains in granite.**
What to use:	**Detergent, water; or bicarb, vinegar, cling film; or plaster of paris, paint brush, plastic/wooden tool, damp cloth.**
How to apply:	Try cleaning the stain with detergent and water first. If this doesn't work, make a paste of bicarb and

vinegar and apply the paste to the stain. Cover it with cling film until it's almost dry. The grease should scrub out with detergent and water. You can also use plaster of paris. Mix to the consistency of peanut butter, then paint the paste over the stain and leave it until it goes hard. Remove the mixture with a plastic or wooden tool so you don't scratch the surface. Rub the rest off with a damp cloth. The plaster pulls the stains out because it's very absorbent.

Stainless steel

The best way to clean stainless steel is with bicarb and vinegar. Dust with bicarb, then splash some vinegar and wipe with a sponge. Rinse with water and wipe with a cloth to remove any smears. Repeat if necessary.

Problem:	**Scratches in stainless steel.**
What to use:	*Gumption*, **sponge, bicarb, vinegar, cloth.**
How to apply:	Apply a dab of *Gumption* to a sponge and rub it over the scratch. This will smooth the surface. Then sprinkle bicarb over the scratch and splash a little vinegar. Remove with a cloth.

Wood

If the wood is unsealed, clean it with detergent and water then dry. Then wipe it with good quality furniture oil. For surfaces that come into contact with food, use a small quantity of warm olive oil. Some olive oils contain vegetable sediment, which can attract fruit flies, so make sure you spread it thinly and wipe off all the excess. Only use olive oil on surfaces in the kitchen. Bicarb and vinegar will remove any stains but remember to reapply the olive oil. If you prefer, keep the timber moist and splinter-free by rubbing it with the skin of a lemon. For sealed wood, clean with bicarb and vinegar. Be very careful with polyurethane surfaces because if you scratch them you'll have to reseal them. If you do scratch polyurethane, wipe it with glycerine.

Problem:	**Dents in wood.**
What to use:	**Hot wet sponge, hairdryer.**
How to apply:	Cut a sponge to the size of the dent, wet it in hot water and place it over the dented area only. Leave the sponge for five minutes, take it off and dry the spot with a hairdryer. The wood should have swelled back into place. Don't put hot sponges on any other part of the wood or it will expand it as well.

Problem:	**Gap between wooden worktop and splashback.**
What to use:	**Disposable rubber gloves, mineral turpentine, silicone sealer; or water, matches, candle wax.**
How to apply:	There are a couple of ways you can fix this. Put on disposable rubber gloves and dip the tip of your finger in mineral turpentine. Then feed silicone with your finger into the gap. Another way is to wear disposable rubber gloves, wet the tip of your finger with water, then light a candle and feed the dripping wax in between the worktop and splashback with your finger. Candle wax doesn't last as long as silicone and would need to be replaced every six months but it has the added bonus of being easy to replace if needed.

Q: 'I left a melon on a timber worktop and it went off,' says Steve. 'It's left a green stain on the worktop and eaten through the varnish!'

Problem:	**Rotten melon on wooden worktop.**
What to use:	**Bicarb, vinegar, nylon brush, varnish.**
How to apply:	Clean the excess oxide by sprinkling bicarb over the area, add vinegar and scrub with a nylon brush. Then rinse with water. Allow it to dry and then re-varnish.

Tiles

Tiled worktops need particular care because bacteria can thrive in the grout. Clean tiles and grout by sprinkling bicarb over the surface then splashing vinegar over the top. Wipe with a cloth then rinse. I'd recommend cleaning tiles more often than other surfaces because grout is so absorbent. Use an old toothbrush to get into tricky areas.

Chopping boards

A clean chopping board is a hygienic chopping board! They can be made of wood, plastic or glass and I reckon the bigger the better. Wood should be scrubbed thoroughly after each use with detergent and water and stood up to dry. To prevent splintering, scrub with olive oil and steel wool once a week. Wood has the added benefit of containing a natural antibacterial. Plastic should be cleaned with detergent and water. As soon as it's scuffed, throw it out because scratches harbour bacteria. Clean glass with bicarb and vinegar. To make cleaning around the chopping board easier, put a tea towel underneath it to collect crumbs and food spills. It also makes chopping quieter and there's less chance you'll mark the worktop.

SINK

Most kitchen sinks are made of stainless steel or enamel, although some are now made of polycarbonate or cement. The best cleaning combination is bicarb and vinegar. If the sink is heavily stained use *Gumption*, but be aware that it contains a mild bleaching agent and abrasive. Avoid using borax in the sink because it's quite toxic and, no matter how well you wash it down, you'll have some residue. Don't use abrasives on polycarbonate and always put the cold tap on before the hot tap or it will craze.

Be mindful what you put down the sink. Not only can it be bad for the environment, but you'll also end up creating more work when the sink becomes clogged. Don't put oil, fats, eggs, proteins or starch-based products down it. For fats and oils, re-use an old tin, put a paper towel on the bottom to stop splatter, and collect the waste. When it's full, throw it in the bin.

If you have mildew or bugs under your sink, place some whole cloves and salt inside the cupboard. You could also rub some oil of cloves around the cupboard door edges under the sink. Apply with a cloth.

Problem:	**Scratches in stainless-steel sink.**
What to use:	***Gumption*, sponge, bicarb, vinegar, cloth.**
How to apply:	Apply a dab of *Gumption* to a sponge and rub it over the scratch. This will smooth the surface. Then sprinkle bicarb over the scratch and splash a little vinegar. Polish with a cloth.

Problem: Tarnished brass sink ring.

What to use: Bicarb, vinegar, sponge or brush; or toothpaste, old toothbrush.

How to apply: If the sink is discoloured, apply bicarb and vinegar with a sponge or brush and scrub. If the ring is badly corroded, put a dab of toothpaste on an old toothbrush and scrub it over the sink ring as though you're cleaning your teeth. Rinse with water.

Problem: Leaking pipes under the sink.

What to use: Hemp rope.

How to apply: Untwist some hemp rope so that you have about six threads or fibres. Then undo the nut and wind the hemp fibres around the thread on the pipe to seal it. Screw the nut back on over the hemp fibres. The fibres expand as soon as they become wet and this creates a really good seal. This was the technique used before plumber's tape was invented. Hemp rope is also good for leaks at the bottom of the tap and sink.

Problem: Smells in the sink drain.

What to use: Bicarb, vinegar.

How to apply: Put 1 tablespoon of bicarb down the drain, followed immediately by 120 ml of vinegar. Leave for half an hour. If it's still smelly, do it again. If you have copper or brass pipes, it will smell worse for about half an hour before it gets better. Once it's rinsed through the smell will dissipate.

Problem: Black mould in the silicone behind the sink.

What to use: Bicarb, vinegar, old toothbrush; or silicone remover, sharp knife, silicone or candle wax.

How to apply: First, try sprinkling bicarb over the mould and then splash with vinegar. Scrub with an old toothbrush then rinse off with water. If this doesn't work, you may need to remove the silicone with a special silicone remover or a very sharp knife. Then replace with new silicone or candle wax.

Washing up by hand

The first rule of washing up is to rinse as much food as possible from plates and cutlery. Rather than leaving the tap running, use a small bucket to rinse items. You can also use paper towels to wipe food off. Put a little hot water in your dirty pots to soak them. Then stack everything needing washing on one side of the sink and have your drying rack on the other side of the sink.

The washing water should be hot, but not too hot. Use a small amount of detergent and wear rubber gloves to prevent slippage. The order to wash things up in is:

1. glassware
2. plastics
3. china
4. cutlery
5. serving dishes
6. pots, pans and cooking utensils

If you have a second sink, keep hot water in it and rinse the item after it's been scrubbed. Then stack the item on the drying rack to air dry or be dried with a tea towel. Air drying is more hygienic.

❏ To avoid streaking, glassware is best drained on a tea towel that has been laid out on the worktop.

❑ Don't put good china or good glassware in water hotter than you could leave your hand in.

❑ Never use steel wool on porcelain or china, no matter how dirty it is. It will scratch the surface, making it porous and vulnerable to dirt and bacteria. If there are ingrained marks, clean them with bicarb and vinegar.

❑ Never use a scourer or abrasives on polycarbonate glasses because they will scratch the surface. Instead, soak them in warm water with a little detergent. For bad staining, apply glycerine first then wash in detergent.

❑ To clean your washing gloves, turn them inside out, put them on and wash your hands in soap. Then leave them inside out to dry.

Taps

Taps can be made of stainless steel, chrome, brass or powder coated. Except for powder-coated taps, clean with bicarb and vinegar. To clean the back of taps, use an old pair of pantyhose. Wrap the leg around the tap and move it in a sawing motion backwards and forwards. Powder coating is a form of plastic that is heat sealed onto the surface of metal to colour it. Powder-coated taps are often cream, white or black. Don't use any abrasives on them, just wash with soap and water and always turn your cold tap on first or the powder coating will chip and discolour.

DRAINS

Drains are designed to take things away but they can also provide an entry for other things, such as insects. To stop insects gaining entry, put flyscreen material behind the drain grill. This will prevent blockages as well.

To keep cockroaches away, wipe a solution of salt and water around the drain.

If your drain is blocked, put 60 g of bicarb down, then add 120 ml of vinegar and leave for half an hour. You can also use a proprietary caustic cleaner. However, if your pipes are old and made of iron, using a caustic cleaner could pit the surface of the pipe (caustic is an oxidising agent and eats into iron), which also means it will hold bacteria.

CUPBOARDS

The more often you wipe your cupboards, the cleaner they will stay. If you can, give them a quick wipe every day. And don't forget about the surface on top of the cupboard. As much as you'd like to adopt the 'out of sight, out of mind' approach, the dust which settles here will gradually spread around the rest of the kitchen. Try this homemade solution which I developed through trial and error and which really cuts through the grime.

In a jar, mix 70 g of grated soap, 2 tablespoons of methylated spirits, 120 ml of vinegar and 2 tablespoons of bicarb. Seal the jar and shake it until all the ingredients are dissolved. Then clean the tops of your cupboards with a cloth. It's a very strong solution and could eat into other surfaces so only use it on this not-for-public-viewing area. To cut back on future cleaning, put paper – even newspaper will do – on top of cupboards and change it regularly.

The best time to clean the underside of wall-mounted cupboards is after making soup or boiling the kettle because the steam softens the grease and grime.

The easiest way to clean inside your kitchen drawers is to vacuum them every couple of weeks, then wipe with a damp cloth. If you haven't cleaned them in a while, use bicarb and vinegar, then wipe with a cloth that has been soaked in hot water.

CROCKERY

Most people have plates for everyday use and another set for special
occasions. Crockery can be made of china, porcelain, pottery, glass
or polycarbonate resin. Those in everyday use can be washed in
detergent and water. Never soak pottery as it can lift the glaze. To
prevent your good china chipping and cracking in cupboards, put a
small piece of paper towel in between the plates. This also helps
prevent wear and tear on them. Never put gold-rimmed china in the
microwave or dishwasher.

Problem: **Plates with discoloured crazing.**
What to use: **Effervescing overnight denture soaker.**
How to apply: Add 2 tablets of denture soaker to a sink full of hot
water. Put the plates in the sink and leave overnight.
Rinse them off in clean water then leave them in the
sun, if possible. Dry them very well. No matter what
anyone tells you, do not soak china in bleach. The
bleach can lift the glaze and cause a white powdery
coating that won't go away.

Problem: **Stained teacups/teapots.**
What to use: **Bicarb, vinegar, nylon brush; or methylated
spirits, cotton wool ball, cotton bud or cloth.**
How to apply: Mix 1 teaspoon of bicarb with 1 tablespoon of
vinegar. Rub it inside the teacup or teapot with a
nylon brush. Rinse in clean water. If you have gold
edging on cups, the tannin in tea builds up a scum
over the gilding. Remove it with methylated spirits
applied with a cotton wool ball, cotton bud or cloth.

Problem: Chips in crockery.

What to use: Denture soaker, glycerine; or sapphire nail file, glycerine or heat-resistant superglue.

How to apply: This is only a temporary solution. Clean the plate in a sink full of hot water with 2 tablets of denture soaker added to it. Allow the plate to dry thoroughly in sunlight. Then soak the chip with glycerine to seal it. It's best to throw chipped crockery away because bacteria can get into the porous surface. For special pieces, see a professional restorer. If you have a sharp chip, file with a sapphire nail file (a file which contains ground sapphire and will grind glass) around the edge of the chip, not down or across the chip. Then treat with glycerine. You can also use heat-resistant superglue to seal the chip. If you have grey lines across a plate, it means the seal has gone and dirt has penetrated into the plate. Rather than throw it away, add it to your recycle box to use as a pot plant saucer or something else. See a restorer for valuable pieces.

Salt and pepper

To keep the salt in your shaker loose, add rice to it. To keep pepper loose, use dried peas. Adding dried peas also keeps parmesan cheese loose.

CUTLERY

Wash cutlery in detergent and water. If it's very dirty, stained or has rust spots, use bicarb and vinegar first. Gold cutlery should only be cleaned with bicarb and vinegar.

Brass, copper, silver and pewter cutlery can also be cleaned in an old aluminium saucepan with 60 g of bicarbonate of soda dissolved in 900 ml of hot water. Put the cutlery in and leave it for a few minutes. Don't put your bare hands into the water because they will burn! Wear rubber gloves or use wooden kitchen tools or skewers to manipulate the pieces. Then rinse the cutlery with water and vinegar. Never add water to the aluminium pot after cleaning. Pour the solution out first as it can boil over because of the reaction between the aluminium, baking soda and hot water.

An old-fashioned way to get a glass-like polish on silverware is to rub it with a paste of wheat bran and vinegar. Put cotton gloves or a pair of old cotton socks on your hands to stop the acid from your hands affecting the silver. Clean the paste off, then polish with a cloth. Remove scratches from silverware by rubbing a handful of wheat bran over it with your hand. Don't use proprietary sprays that contain silicone. Clean pewter with wheat bran and vinegar but be careful not to overpolish it or you'll remove the patina of age and devalue the piece.

To clean, polish and seal bone handles on cutlery, mix 20 parts sweet almond oil to 1 part oil of cloves and mix thoroughly. Then rub this mixture over the handles. If the handles have become dry and cracked, leave them soaking in the mixture. After soaking, polish with a clean cloth. If the bone is very dirty, clean it first with bicarb and a little water. Never use heat with bone because it will discolour and crack.

Q: 'I'd like to know how to stop the dishwasher leaving rust on my stainless-steel cutlery,' says Nicole.

Problem:	**Rust on cutlery.**
What to use:	**Bicarb, vinegar.**
How to apply:	The dishwasher sandblasts your cutlery and creates rust marks. Polish the cutlery by hand with a paste of vinegar and bicarb, wipe, then rinse off in water.

Q: 'I've got green marks on my Thai copper cutlery,' says Susan. 'Do they come off?'

Problem:	Green marks on copper cutlery.
What to use:	Bicarb, vinegar, nylon brush.
How to apply:	Lay the cutlery in the sink and sprinkle bicarb over it, then splash vinegar on top. Scrub with a nylon brush and rinse. The reason Thais use copper cutlery is because curries taste sweeter when eaten with copper. Silver gives curries an acidic tang.

KNIVES

When I was young, I remember seeing a Chinese chef creating sculptures out of vegetables with his Chinese chopper. It was a fantastic sight to witness. I later learned that half the skill lies in having a good knife! Choose the best you can afford. I suggest using a Chinese chopper, a large carving knife, a carving knife with a curved blade, a serrated bread knife, a serrated vegetable knife and a paring knife. Choose high-quality steel and ensure handles are solid and well secured.

If you use the wrong tools to sharpen knives, they'll rust. Only sharpen them with a steel and a whetstone. Never use cheap wheel sharpeners or you'll demagnetise the blades and get rust spots. If in doubt, use a professional knife sharpener. I suggest asking your local restaurant when their knife sharpener is coming and arranging to have yours sharpened at the same time. Never use steel wool to clean a knife because it'll rust.

GLASSWARE

The worst things for glass are extreme heat, extreme cold, chemicals and abrasives. To protect your good glassware, avoid putting it in the dishwasher. As I've said before, I hate dishwashers, particularly when it comes to glass because it becomes scratched and cloudy-looking and this damage is permanent. Don't soak glassware in detergents or use strong bleach products. Just use water.

To prevent crystal becoming cloudy, only wash it in water no hotter than you can leave your hands in. Add a small amount of white vinegar to the wash to prevent spotting and fogging.

To clean dirt out of champagne glasses or glassware that has narrow apertures, put a little olive oil in the glass first and leave for a few minutes. The oil collects and lifts the dust. Then get a thin, long-handled paintbrush, wrap sticky tape around the ferrule, or silver part, and rub it around the difficult-to-reach area. Wash the glasses in detergent and water. If it's too narrow for a thin paint-brush, use a bamboo skewer and chew the end of it until it's shaped like a brush.

- ❏ Always put a tea towel in the bottom of the sink in case you drop a piece while your hands are wet. The tea towel will cushion the impact.
- ❏ Never leave wine sitting in glasses because it will leave a mark.
- ❏ To remove lipstick on the edge of glasses, dip a small cotton wool ball in vinegar and wipe over the lipstick.
- ❏ Never twist a tea towel through a stemmed glass as the glass could snap.

Problem:	Soap scum on glass.
What to use:	**Vinegar, water, cloth.**
How to apply:	Mix 1 tablespoon of vinegar with 240 ml of water. Place the glass in the mixture. Then polish dry with a cloth.

Q: Gabrielle puts everything in the dishwasher. 'But I've noticed I'm getting white marks on my glasses. What can I do about this?'

Problem:	**Whiteness on glass.**
What to use:	**Goanna oil.**
How to apply:	If it's soap scum, see above. If it's been scratched, the damage is permanent. You may be able to alleviate the problem by soaking it in goanna oil; however, this only works on some pieces and you don't know which ones will respond until you do it. Leave the goanna oil on for a week.

Problem:	**Tiny chips on the edge of your glass.**
What to use:	**Sapphire nail file.**
How to apply:	Place the nail file horizontally and flat to the rim of the glass and slowly buff along the chips. Never go across or down the glass.

How to remove sticky labels

I come from a family that always removed labels from jars before putting them on the table because it was considered the polite thing to do. And, because it was the era before tupperware and takeaway containers, we used glass jars for everything! There are several ways to remove sticky labels from glass and plastic containers. One method is to fill them with hot

water, close the lid tightly and leave for a few minutes. Then lift the edge of the sticker slowly with a blunt knife. If any adhesive remains, wipe it with tea-tree oil. Another way is to lay down a piece of cling film just bigger than the sticker. Mix one drop of detergent with a small quantity of water in a spray pack, spray it over the cling film then place the cling film over the sticker. Leave for five minutes, or longer if the glue is very strong. The sticker will come off with the cling film. Rubbing dry-cleaning fluid or eucalyptus oil over the label, then rubbing off again, are other alternatives. Just make sure you neutralise them afterwards with methylated spirits. Don't try to remove the label by placing the jar itself into hot water—even though the paper will dissolve, the glue won't and you'll be left with a sticky mess that you'll have to rub and rub and rub!

THE PANTRY

Because I was one of five children I learned to cook from an early age. The first thing I ever cooked was baked apples and cinnamon. I've always enjoyed cooking and experimenting with flavours and this is much easier to do if your pantry is organised.

If you organise your pantry by keeping similar items together, you won't waste time searching for things. If you don't have enough room in your pantry, think about putting another shelf in. Or get some free-standing wire shelves that are stackable.

Keep grain foods separately because bugs are attracted to them. Once you open any packet, put the contents in an air-tight container and mark the contents and use-by date on it. I like to cut the relevant information from the packet and sticky tape or glue it to the jar. You can also seal a packet with an old bread clip or bulldog clip. Putting a bay leaf in containers will help keep moths and weevils away. Another way to prevent weevils in grain food is to make a small cling film bag, fill it full of salt, seal the top and prick the bag with pinholes. Place this inside the containers. I always remove cereals from the cardboard box because insects are attracted to cardboard. Seal the plastic liner with a peg or old bread clip.

Most canned food will last from two to four years, but the earlier you consume it, the better. Most cans have a use-by date on them. If they don't, write the date of purchase on the side. I learned the hard way when a can exploded in the pantry. It's an experience I don't want to repeat any time soon!

Refrigerate jars such as mayonnaise and mustard after opening.

Oils will go off and become rancid. You should only store them for about six months. Rather than buying expensive oil sprays, put oil in your own spray pack. Oils react differently when heated and some leave more grease than others on your kitchen cupboards. Rapeseed oil is the worst for leaving oily scum as it seems to fume more. I bought a cheap drum of it once thinking it was a bargain but it was costly in cleaning-up terms! However, it's great as a salad oil or for low-temperature cooking. As a rule, the better the quality of oil, the less splattering you're likely to get. Have a range of oils available so you use the right oil for the job. For example, don't use olive oil for chips because the oil will burn before the chips are cooked.

Place a layer of paper towel in the bottom of a sugar container to prevent lumping and clumping. If you put a piece of terracotta in your brown sugar it won't clot.

Always keep your dried herbs tightly sealed in glass or plastic and out of strong sunlight. Buy them in small quantities because they lose their flavour after about six months. Even better, grow them fresh on your windowsill.

Q: 'We've got these pesky moths in the pantry that seem to breed in anything and everything,' says Michael. 'Can we get rid of them?'

Problem:	**Moths in the pantry.**
What to use:	**Oil of pennyroyal or bay oil or mint tea, cloth.**
How to apply:	Put 1 drop of oil of pennyroyal in a bucket of water, then wipe the shelves with a cloth. **Don't use oil of pennyroyal if you're pregnant.** Pregnant women can apply bay oil to a cloth and then wipe over the shelves or they can wipe the shelves with a very strong mint tea. These methods aren't as effective as oil of pennyroyal and have to be reapplied more often but they will work.

Recycling containers

Nearly everything we buy comes in a container. Hang on to these because there are plenty of other ways you can use them. For example, plastic takeaway containers can be reused for leftovers. To get rid of the greasy feel, put a little vinegar in the water when you're rinsing. Even cereal boxes can be converted into files for paperwork. Plastic bags can be washed, hung out and reused. Reuse tins to store nails and other things. Hold on to jars as well, as they're good for storing liquids.

Sweet-smelling hands

Rubbing your hands with bicarb and vinegar removes smells, especially after working with onions, garlic or chilli. An alternative is to wear disposable gloves when chopping.

The Bathroom

Bathrooms seem to be multiplying as fast as rabbits.

The absolute minimum now appears to be

two, master bedrooms must have an ensuite and

larger homes have as many bathrooms as

bedrooms. And let's not forget the toilet and shower

downstairs! We want all of these to be immaculate.

And not just for us; no one wants guests discovering a

mouldy ceiling, dirty tiles or something worse in one of

our many ablution centres.

I've cleaned many a bathroom in my time! But I quite

enjoy it because it's a room designed to be cleaned.

The surfaces are easy to access and leave a sparkle

so I always feel a sense of satisfaction afterwards.

Remember: always work from top to bottom.

BE CAREFUL WHERE YOU PUT SPRAY CANS: DEBORAH'S STORY

Incident: 'I've got a beautiful old marble vanity top. But the look of it is marred by some circles of rust that I can't remove. It's such a pity because the marble is so beautiful. Is there any way of removing them?'

Solution: Put a circle of bicarb over the rust mark, add vinegar and rub it off with a sponge. The rust stains were probably caused by the bottom of a hairspray can. Most cans are unsealed, and when they interact with water, they rust. One way to prevent this is to paint clear nail polish on the bottom of any cans that sit on the vanity top. You could also keep a small wooden tray on your vanity top for storing unsealed cans, or go old-fashioned and use doilies.

Q: 'We've got a problem with millipedes,' says Helen. 'They head for the bathroom and create a massive black mess.'

Problem: Millipedes in the bathroom.
What to use: Oil of pennyroyal, cloth.
How to apply: Put a couple of drops of oil of pennyroyal on a cloth and wipe it over the areas where the millipedes crawl. **Never use oil of pennyroyal if you're pregnant**.

Q: 'I've got these little black flying bugs in my bathroom,' reports Sam. 'They gravitate towards the roof. Is there anything I can do?'

Problem: Black bugs in bathroom.
What to use: Salt, water, sponge.

How to apply: These could be a variety of fruit bugs. Many shampoos have fruit oil in them, which attracts some bugs. Make sure your shampoo is sealed and keep the tops of the containers clean. If the bugs are beetles, make a solution of salt and water and paint it around your drains and windowsills with a sponge.

TOILET

Has anyone shown you how to clean the toilet properly? I'll assume 'no' was the answer to that question. This is my approach using bicarb and vinegar, but feel free to substitute the cleaning product of your choice.

Tools: **Bicarb, sponges, vinegar, toilet brush.**

Technique:
1. Flush the toilet to wet the sides of the bowl.
2. Sprinkle bicarb over the inside of the bowl.
3. Wipe the top of the cistern using the two-sponge technique with bicarb and vinegar.
4. Wipe the top of the lid, under the lid, the top of the seat and under the seat using the same technique.
5. Splash vinegar over the bicarb in the bowl, then use a toilet brush to scrub, including up and around the rim.
6. Wipe the top of the rim with a sponge.
7. Wash the sponge in hot water and wipe again.
8. Flush.
9. Rinse the sponge and wipe the outside of the toilet bowl right to the floor, including the plumbing at the back.
10. Congratulations, you're done!

The ping-pong ball technique

If you have a young boy who's having difficulty getting all his pee in the bowl, put a ping-pong ball at the bottom of the toilet and tell him to aim for it. The ping-pong ball won't flush because it's too light and you'll be surprised at how much better his aim becomes.

Problem: **Bad stains on the inside of the toilet bowl.**
What to use: **Small plastic cup, bicarb, vinegar, nylon brush.**
How to apply: Turn the tap off at the cistern. Drain the bottom of the bowl with a small plastic cup. Then sprinkle bicarb over the bowl and splash some vinegar over the bicarb. Scrub with a nylon brush. Turn the water back on at the cistern.

Q: 'We've got orange rust stains on our toilet bowl from bore water,' says Sue. 'How can we remove them?'

Problem: **Rust stains/hard-water fur.**
What to use: **Descaler, rubber gloves, mask.**
How to apply: Put half a cap of descaler into the cistern, leave it for an hour, then flush the toilet. This will help prevent the bowl staining as it cleans the fur out of the cistern. For heavy stains, clean the bowl with descaler but make sure you use rubber gloves and a mask. Note that descaler should only be used to remove staining and not as a regular cleaner.

Problem: **Dirty seat.**
What to use: **Bicarb, vinegar, sponge; or *Gumption*; and sweet almond oil or glycerine.**

How to apply:	For plastic seats, sprinkle bicarb then wipe a vinegar-soaked sponge over the top. For bakelite seats, put a dab of *Gumption* on a sponge and wipe it over the seat. Then rinse with water. If you've lost that glossy look on your bakelite toilet seat, rub a drop of sweet almond oil on it. If it's plastic, rub it with glycerine.
Problem:	**Urine smell.**
What to use:	**A lemon, ice-cream container, water; or vinegar, water.**
How to apply:	Wash surfaces with the juice from half a lemon added to an ice-cream container of water. Alternatively, use vinegar and water. Lemon is preferable because it leaves a nice smell. It's particularly important to wipe the pipes at the back of the toilet.
Problem:	**Rubber beginning to perish.**
What to use:	**Salt, glycerine, talcum powder, cloth.**
How to apply:	Rub the perish marks with salt, wipe over with glycerine and then sprinkle with talcum powder. When dry, remove the talcum powder with a cloth. If the rubber has perished too much, you'll need to replace it.

Cutting back on toilet paper

I grew up in a house with more girls than boys and we went through loads of toilet paper. If you have the same problem, squash the roll before you put it on the roller. This slows the spin down and stops little fingers making paper trails through the house.

Non-toxic air freshener

I suffer from asthma and proprietary sprays make me wheeze so I created this non-toxic bathroom air freshener. Fill a spray pack with water and add 2 drops of detergent and 5 drops of lavender oil. You can substitute other essential oils except those with high colouring levels, such as stone fruits. Eucalyptus oil should be used sparingly because it will mark painted surfaces. Spray as needed.

BATH

Taking a bath is one of life's great luxuries. My Mother's Day treat is taking a bath with a glass of champagne, my favourite book and no one bothering me.

Most baths are made of vitreous china although new ones are made of acrylic, fibreglass or polycarbonate. You may also encounter stainless-steel, metal or cast-iron baths. Use bicarb and vinegar to clean them or, if they're very dirty, *Gumption*. An old pair of stockings rolled into a ball is great to clean with because it cuts through soap scum really well without scratching. Never use steel wool to clean baths or you'll leave scratch marks.

If you have a cast-iron bath, don't put hot water in first. Cast iron shrinks and expands at a different rate to the enamel covering and if the water is too hot you'll get chips and cracks. Put a little cold water in cast-iron and polycarbonate baths first.

When cleaning the bath, clean the tiles above the bath first, then the taps, then the sides and bottom of the bath. Then rinse. Never use abrasives on polycarbonate baths. Use glycerine to remove stains.

Problem:	**Rust stains on the sink ring.**
What to use:	**Rubber gloves, descaler, cloth.**
How to apply:	Put on rubber gloves then wipe descaler on the sink ring with a cloth. Wipe it off then rinse.

Problem:	**Scratches in fibreglass.**
What to use:	**Glycerine, 2000-grade wet-and-dry.**
How to apply:	Put glycerine on the wet-and-dry and rub over the scratch.

Spa baths

At the press of a button, a bath is transformed into a bubbling comfort zone. Clean spa baths the same way as regular baths but look out for chalk deposits, body fat and skin cell build-up. Chalk deposits come about because soap and water is flushed backwards and forwards at different temperatures. Remove with vinegar and clean the nozzle regularly with descaler. After every couple of uses, run vinegar and water through the spa.

SHOWER

It might be OK to wear thongs in the shower at a caravan park but do you really want to do this in your own home? Keep the area clean with bicarb and vinegar. Sprinkle bicarb over the surfaces then splash some vinegar over the top and wipe with a sponge or brush. Then rinse with water. For vertical surfaces, have a tray with some bicarb in it and a bucket with vinegar in it and use two separate sponges. Begin with the bicarb sponge then press the vinegar sponge over the bicarb sponge and wipe. Rinse with water. If you have particularly grimy surfaces, use *Gumption*. If you like fragrance, add a couple of drops of tea-tree oil, lavender oil or eucapytus oil to the rinse water. Don't use eucalyptus oil on anything plastic or painted.

Problem: **Soap scum build-up in soap holder.**
What to use: **Old pair of stockings, warm water.**
How to apply: Scrub the soap scum with an old pair of stockings
                   rolled into a ball and warm water.

Shower screen

As a general rule, it's best not to use abrasives or strong chemicals
on any shower screens. If you have a glass shower screen, clean it
with bicarb and vinegar like the rest of the shower. Some shower
screens have nylon and wire in between two layers of glass, and
problems occur because air cavities are created. This allows
moisture to get in and causes either mould or glass cancer on the
inside of the screen. It often looks as though you've got soap scum
on the screen. I've seen this many times and unfortunately there's
not much you can do about it. You can alleviate the scratchiness
with goanna oil, which you rub over the surface and edges. If you
can't live with the scratchiness, you'll have to buy a new screen or
get some glass-etching cream and make the clouds a feature. The
other common type of shower screen is made of polycarbonate and
should only be cleaned with vinegar.

Q: 'I find that my shower screen becomes streaky,'
says Kaye. 'What do you suggest?'

Problem: **Streaky shower screen.**
What to use: **Methylated spirits, vinegar, water, cloth.**
How to apply: Mix 1 part methylated spirits with 1 part vinegar and
                   2 parts water. The amount you need depends on
                   how big the screen is. Rub the mixture over the
                   screen with a cloth.

Problem:	**Mould in silicone join.**
What to use:	**Bicarb, vinegar, old toothbrush; or new silicone.**
How to apply:	Mix the bicarb and vinegar into a paste and apply with an old toothbrush. Try this a few times. If it doesn't shift, you'll need to replace the silicone.

Shower curtain

Constant moisture and poor ventilation make the shower curtain a prime candidate for mould. Whether it's plastic or nylon, wash the curtain in the washing machine on the cool cycle once a fortnight. To prevent further mildew, add a drop of oil of cloves to the rinse water of the washing machine.

Shower head

If the water in your shower head sprays in different directions, it's likely you've got hard-water fur. If you can see little black prickly things coming out of the nozzle, that's also hard-water fur. To get rid of it, use descaler. Mix descaler according to the directions on the packet in a bucket or old ice cream container. Hold the container so that the shower head is completely immersed. Keep it there until the solution is absorbed. This should take a few minutes. Then turn on the shower: the black prickles will drop out and go down the drain. You can also unscrew the shower head and clean it inside the ice cream container with descaler.

TAPS

You always create a good impression if your taps are clean and shiny. Taps can be made of stainless steel, brass, copper, chrome or powder coated. The best way to clean them is with bicarb and vinegar, except powder-coated taps. Powder coating is a form of plastic that is heat sealed onto the surface of metal to colour it. It often comes in cream, white and black. Don't use abrasives, just wash with soap and water. An old pair of stockings is the easiest way to clean taps. Wrap them around the tap and saw backwards and forwards.

TILES

Clean tiles once a week with bicarb and vinegar. Have one sponge with bicarb on it and the other with vinegar on it and put the vinegar-soaked sponge over the top of the bicarb-coated sponge, then wipe. The grout between the tiles is very porous and retains mildew. To clean it, use bicarb and vinegar and scrub with an old toothbrush. To inhibit mould, add a couple of drops of oil of cloves to the mixture. You should clean the grout every couple of months to avoid build-up.

There is another way to keep mould under control but you may baulk at this suggestion. Keep a couple of slugs! Slugs will happily eat mould. They sleep during the day so if you create a little house for them, you won't step on them while showering!

MIRROR

When I learned that scuba divers keep their goggles clear by spitting into them, I tested this on the bathroom mirror and found that spit stops the mirror from fogging. Just spit onto a tissue and wipe it over the mirror. If this doesn't appeal to you, write on the mirror with pure soap then polish vigorously with a slightly damp paper towel. I discovered this at an Ideal Home Show where a man was selling 'Magic Mirror Demisting Sticks'. They turned out to be just soap. Clean the mirror with methylated spirits and a paper towel.

HAND BASIN AND VANITY UNIT

Clean the hand basin and vanity with bicarb and vinegar. Sprinkle bicarb over the surface, then wipe with a vinegar-soaked sponge. Clean cupboards and shelving the same way. To prevent bottles breaking in your drawers, line them with a thin piece of foam rubber. This cushions any drops and makes cleaning the drawers easier.

Problem: **Mildew on vanity cupboard.**
What to use: **Salt, bucket, hot water, oil of cloves, sponge.**
How to apply: Dissolve 225 g of salt in a bucket of hot water. Add 2 drops of oil of cloves. Wipe this on the inside of the vanity with a sponge. This will also help to keep insects away.

TOWELS

Q: 'I've got bath towels with tar-like marks on them,' says Diane. 'It's just a strange black mess.'

Problem: **Rubber on towels.**
What to use: **Baby oil, dry-cleaning fluid, cotton wool ball.**
How to apply: The black marks are probably decomposing rubber from the washing machine seals or plumbing. Soften the stain first with baby oil, then apply dry-cleaning fluid with a cotton wool ball. Wash normally.

BATHROOM WALLS

Moisture and poor ventilation are generally the reasons painted bathroom walls go mouldy. Leave the window open as much as possible and use ceiling vents. Each time you clean, add 2 drops of oil of cloves to your rinse water and wipe the walls. Oil of cloves will prevent mould growing and makes the walls easier to clean. It also has a nice fresh smell.

Q: 'We're repainting our bathroom walls,' reports James. 'At the moment, there's quite a bit of mould on them. Is there anything we can use to stop the mould coming back once we've painted?'

Problem:	**Mould on painted walls.**
What to use:	**Hospital-grade bleach, bicarb, vinegar, sponge.**
How to apply:	Because the mould is so severe, clean the surface twice with hospital-grade bleach. Then wipe bicarb and vinegar over the walls with a sponge before you paint them to neutralise the bleach. Also use a mould inhibitor such as oil of cloves or a proprietary product before and during the painting.

Lounge, Dining and Family Rooms

These rooms are all about flow. The lounge flows into the dining room and into the family room, then out onto the patio, around by the barbecue and out into the garden. It's a great way to live, but it means that eating, drinking, playing and socialising are happening all through these spaces. Someone is going to spill their latte on the sofa, an adorable child is going to smear paint over the floor, battalions of muddy shoes are going to mark their path to the TV. Relax! Smile like they do in the cleaning commercials on TV, because we can fix everything!

UNWANTED WATER MARK: RUTH'S STORY

Incident: 'I have a beautiful antique Chinese opium table that my friend's mother bought in China. But I very foolishly put a vase of flowers on it not knowing the vase was porous. It's left a horrible whitish stain on the table. I've tried to clean it with furniture polish but you can still see a pale circle.'

Solution: Warm some beeswax in the microwave or put the tin in a bowl of warm water to soften it. Once softened, add a little turpentine to the warmed wax and apply it to the table with a piece of lemon peel, using the outer, yellow side of the peel. Remove the interior of the lemon first so you don't get any juice on the table. Rub the outside of the lemon peel over the stain as though you were polishing with a cloth. Lemon peel contains a very fine oil which acts as a cleaner and is also a mild bleaching agent. Then rub the oil off with a cloth. You may need to do this a couple of times before the white ring is removed. If you need to reseal it, use a water-impermeable shellac.

SOFA CARE

I often sew while sitting on the sofa but learned the hard way not to use the armrest as a pincushion! Vacuum once a week, making sure to clean under and behind cushions. If you're lucky, you might even find some spare change. Cotton, wool or blended sofas can be cleaned with upholstery or carpet cleaner. I've found that carpet cleaner is preferable because it's a drier foam and the less water you use the better. Always test a patch first to see if it's colour-fast. Put a damp cloth, such as a white towel, onto a section of the fabric and rub a warm iron over it. If any colour comes off on the towel, it's not colour-fast and you can't use an upholstery or carpet cleaner. Instead, clean with bran in a process described later in this chapter or go to a professional cleaner. You can also test colour-fastness by putting vinegar on a cloth and rubbing the upholstery. If any colour is transferred to the cloth, it's not colour-fast. Just make sure you test in an inconspicuous spot.

Every couple of months, remove all cushions and turn the sofa upside down. Vacuum any bugs and discover lost items, as I did with a ring once. If you find spider webs under the sofa, wipe the corners with some lemon oil to deter future spiders. Insecticide spray works as well, though not everyone likes the fumes.

If yours is a house with four-legged friends, get rid of fur and hair by putting on disposable rubber gloves. Then wash your gloved hands with soap and water. This removes the powder from the gloves. Shake your gloved hands dry and drag them over the fur and hair on the sofa. The water on the gloves makes them statically charged and the rubber draws the fur away. I learned this trick after an Old English sheepdog followed me home. It was the hairiest dog I've ever come across and always seemed to drop white hair on dark colours and black hair on light colours. The poor thing had so much hair it used to cough up hairballs. We had the dog until we moved back to the city and found it a new home.

With food spills, always clean up as much as you can with paper towels, working from the outside to the inside of the spill. Remember to remove protein stains first with detergent suds and **a little** cold water, and then deal with fat stains with detergent suds and **a little** hot water. If you remove the fats first, you set the proteins and the task becomes so much harder. If in doubt, always treat the stain as though it has protein in it and use cold water first. If they're just grime stains, use bran and vinegar.

After washing cushion covers, put them back on when they're almost dry but just slightly damp. They'll be easier to put back on because the fibres are relaxed. No need to iron!

To avoid vacuum-cleaner marks on fabric, put an old T-shirt or cloth over the end of the tube or head of the vacuum cleaner and secure with an elastic band. Scotchguarding furniture adds another layer of protection and prevents stains.

COTTON FABRIC

Many people ask how to remove pen stains from fabric. The first thing you need to establish is what kind of ink is in the pen, which will be written on the pen. It's either water-based or spirit-based ink or permanent ink. The treatment is very different, as outlined below.

Q: 'My three-year-old got hold of a black permanent pen and wrote all over the cream furniture,' reports Melinda. 'It's a disaster!'

Problem:	Permanent pen on fabric.
What to use:	Dry-cleaning fluid, cotton bud, cotton wool ball; or hairspray, cloth.
How to apply:	You'll need to do this very carefully and quickly. Apply some dry-cleaning fluid to a cotton bud and write over the permanent pen while also quickly wiping the dry-cleaning fluid off with a cotton wool ball, replacing it often. You could also spray it with hairspray, and wipe off with a cloth. Be careful with the fabric and test a patch first.

Problem:	**Ink stain on fabric.**
What to use:	**Milk, detergent, water; or dry-cleaning fluid, cotton wool ball, talcum powder.**
How to apply:	Rot the milk by leaving it in the sun until solids form. The time this takes varies according to the weather and the age of the milk. Place the solids on the stain, leave until you see the ink start to rise up in the solids, then wash the solids out using detergent and water. You can also use dry-cleaning fluid applied with a cotton wool ball on either side of the stain. If you can't get underneath the stain, sprinkle talcum powder over the dry-cleaning fluid to absorb it.
Problem:	**Rust stains on fabric.**
What to use:	**Descaler, water, cotton wool ball, cotton bud; or salt, lemon juice; or salt, vinegar, cloth, water.**
How to apply:	Only use descaler if you can get to both sides of the fabric, as you must be able to rinse it off. Dilute 1 part descaler to 20 parts water. Hold a cotton wool ball on the non-stained side of the fabric and apply diluted descaler to the rust stain with a cotton bud. You will see the rust loosen from the fibres. Then rinse thoroughly with water. For a natural alternative, put salt on the rust then add lemon juice. Leave it to dry then repeat. It could take a few attempts before the rust shifts. Another option is a salt and vinegar solution. Mix them together to form a thick paste and apply it to the rust mark. When the rust bleeds into the fabric, rinse with water.

Q: 'I've got an armchair with a cotton valance around the bottom of it and it's got scuff marks from people's shoes on it. How do I get the marks off?' asks Lisa.

Problem: Scuff marks on fabric.

What to use: Dry-cleaning fluid, cotton wool balls, methylated spirits or detergent suds.

How to apply: Apply dry-cleaning fluid to the scuff marks with a cotton wool ball. Use clean cotton wool balls on either side of the fabric and work the top cotton wool ball from the outside to the inside of the stain. If the dry-cleaning fluid leaves a smell, neutralise it with either methylated spirits or detergent suds.

Q: 'My children were playing with lipstick and got some over the fabric ottoman,' reports Magda. 'Can I get it off?'

Problem: Lipstick on fabric.

What to use: Glycerine, cotton wool ball.

How to apply: Put some glycerine on a cotton wool ball and wipe from the outside to the inside of the stain. Just make sure you don't get the fabric too wet.

Q: 'My husband likes to read the newspaper in an armchair. But I've noticed that it has become really grubby on the arms from the newspaper ink. It's covered in a cream cotton fabric. Is there anything I can do?' asks June.

Problem:	**Dirty marks on fabric.**
What to use:	**Vinegar, sponge, wheat bran, handkerchief or muslin cloth; or bran, vinegar, bowl, soft brush.**
How to apply:	For lighter marks, gently damp the dirty section of the chair with vinegar on a sponge. Then wrap some bran in a handkerchief or muslin cloth and rub it over the damp section. For dirtier marks, dampen the bran with vinegar in a bowl until it just starts to clump together (add vinegar one drop at a time and mix thoroughly). The bran grains should be clumping, but not wet or sticky. If the fabric is really dirty, damp the whole area with vinegar, then throw raw bran over the top and sweep backwards and forwards with a soft brush. Bran is a scourer and very absorbent.

Problem:	**Oily stain on fabric.**
What to use:	**Detergent, water, cloth or old toothbrush, paper towel.**
How to apply:	The best way to remove oily stains from absorbent fabric is with lots of detergent suds and a little water. Rub the suds into the oil with a cloth or an old tooth-brush, blot with a paper towel, a fine-grade, chamois-like block, and allow it to dry out. The detergent suds help to break down fats and bring them to the surface. You may need to repeat this process a few times to completely shift the oil.

Problem:	**Cigarette smells in furniture.**
What to use:	**Bicarb, wooden spoon, vacuum cleaner.**
How to apply:	Sprinkle the upholstery with bicarbonate of soda then beat it with a wooden spoon. Once you've finished beating, vacuum the bicarb off.

BROCADE

Brocade is an intricately woven fabric made from any fibre. The weave is very fine so special care must be taken when cleaning it. Use vinegar and bran as for 'Dirty marks on fabric' on page 68 to clean it, or go to a professional cleaner.

Q: 'I was lucky enough to inherit my granny's antique chair, which is covered in brocade. But she must have had a leaking hot-water bottle because the chair is covered in water stains. What should I do?' asks Brenda.

Problem:	Water marks in fabric.
What to use:	Sponge, vinegar, bran, muslin; or clean handkerchief, soft brush, vacuum cleaner.
How to apply:	Dampen the water marks with a sponge soaked in vinegar, then wrap some bran in muslin or a clean handkerchief and wipe it over the vinegar. If the stains are really stubborn, you may need to apply the bran directly. Heap it over the vinegar, brush with a soft brush then vacuum off.

VELVET

In the 1960s, velvet was really fashionable. I used to go to furniture upholsterers and use their offcuts to create clothes, particularly waistcoats. But velvet is one of the hardest fabrics to clean. Start by trying to remove as much fluff as possible. Wear rubber gloves, wash your hands in soapy water, shake dry and rub the gloves over the velvet. The fluff should stick to the gloves. After you've removed as much as possible, give the velvet a light spray with a carpet cleaner. Leave it to dry then vacuum the carpet cleaner off.

Problem: Grease stain on velvet.

What to use: Bicarb, bristle brush, vacuum cleaner.

How to apply: Sprinkle the stain with bicarb then brush it gently backwards and forwards with a bristle brush, not a nylon brush. Leave it for 10 minutes then vacuum or brush firmly.

Q: 'I've got a water mark on my velvet sofa which has made the velvet bits go all hard and bristly,' says Belinda. 'Can it be repaired?'

Problem: Water mark on velvet.

What to use: Bowl, bran, vinegar, brush, vacuum cleaner.

How to apply: In a bowl, mix bran with drops of vinegar until it's just damp but not clumpy. Then apply the mixture to the water mark with your fingers and leave for a few minutes. Brush the area in circles and leave to dry. Then vacuum the bran.

Problem: Bald patch in velvet.

What to use: Matches, stranded cotton or silk, tufting tool.

How to apply: First, you need to determine what the velvet is made of. Test a patch along a seam using the head of a hot match. If the fabric smells like burnt hair, it's cotton or silk. If it smells of plastic, it's polyester. Cotton has a matt finish. Silk has a high sheen. Find matching fabric, then use a tufting tool to stab and loop the fibres through the bald patch. (Tufting tools come with easy instructions but practise on a scrap piece of fabric first.) Then trim the cotton or silk threads to the same height as the velvet with sharp scissors. Embroidery or manicure scissors should do the job.

TAPESTRY

I used to do a lot of tapestries and petit point. The best way to clean tapestry is with dry bran. Put a handful into a muslin cloth bag, heat it in the microwave for half a minute, then rub it over the tapestry. The bran will absorb the dirt. You can also apply the bran directly. Firstly, slightly moisten it with vinegar. Add one drop at a time until it forms clumps like couscous, but not a ball. Sprinkle this across the stain, rub backwards and forwards with a cloth or soft brush, then vacuum it off.

Q:

'I've got a piano stool that is covered in a wool tapestry,' says Shirley. 'It was a wedding gift from my aunt 50 years ago. And after years of use, you can hardly see the flowers any more. Can it be cleaned?'

Problem: Dirty tapestry.

What to use: Wheat bran; or heavy cotton, woolwash, bucket.

How to apply: Try cleaning it with bran as outlined above. If that doesn't work, test it for colour-fastness by soaking a white cloth in vinegar and applying to a small, less noticeable portion of the tapestry. If any colour comes off, it is not colour-fast. If it *is* colour-fast, remove the tapestry from the stool and stitch it to a piece of heavy cotton. Hand wash it in 1 teaspoon of woolwash or shampoo added to a bucket of blood-heat water, then completely rinse the piece in blood-heat water before drying it in the shade. You can unstitch the cotton backing or leave it on. Either way, replace the tapestry on the stool while the cotton is still slightly damp because it will have more stretch. If it's not colour-fast, take it to a restorer.

You can make your own woolwash with 2 tablespoons of pure soap flakes, $1/2$ cup of cheap hair conditioner and 2–3 drops of eucalyptus oil. Mix with a little warm water or put into a jar and shake. One teaspoon of this mixture is enough for a bucket of jumpers.

LEATHER

Clean leather sofas once a week with either saddle soap or leather dew. Keep a dedicated cloth in a plastic snap-lock bag for this purpose. Never use water to clean leather because it stiffens it. And always secure a cloth or T-shirt over the vacuum-cleaner head to prevent scratches in the leather. Most stains can be removed with dry-cleaning fluid. After applying the fluid with a cotton wool ball, sprinkle talcum powder to absorb it. Brush off the talcum powder when it's dry and treat with leather dew or saddle soap. Never use toothpaste as it can leave dry, rough or bleached spots.

Problem:	**Dog and cat scratches in dark brown leather.**
What to use:	**Walnut; or shoe cream, cloth, leather dew; or camphor, mothballs and holder, lavender oil or lavender bags.**
How to apply:	Remove the walnut from its shell, if it has one, and cut it in half. Then rub the cut walnut over the scratch so that its oils coat the scratch. Leave for 1 hour for the colour to cure. If the sofa isn't brown leather, choose an appropriately coloured shoe cream but not shoe polish or wax. Apply the shoe cream with a cloth. It only feeds the areas that need it. After that, apply leather dew with a cloth to soften.

To prevent more scratches, scatter camphor at the back of the sofa, underneath the cushions, to deter a cat. You could also tuck a mothball holder between the cushions. Use lavender oil or lavender bags behind the seat cushions to deter a dog.

Q:

'I was making a correction really quickly,' says Jill, 'and accidentally spilled white correction fluid on a leather armchair. Is it removeable?'

Problem:	**White correction fluid on leather.**
What to use:	**White correction fluid remover, leather dew.**
How to apply:	Apply the white correction fluid remover then resurface immediately with leather dew.

CANE, BAMBOO AND WICKER FURNITURE

Cane tends to be a very popular restoration item. Our family has a set of early Victorian cane baby furniture that has been passed from family to family. The best way to clean cane, bamboo and wicker is to mix 2 teaspoons of bicarb in 1 litre of water and rub it over the furniture with a sponge, then rinse. Dab some baby oil on a cloth to polish.

How to fix a hole in cane furniture

Use some matching or similar cane that is longer than the hole you're repairing. Make it into single canes and soak them in hot water. Reweave the cane starting where the original cane is still solid. Don't cut the old pieces until it's been rewoven. Tuck the ends in and down at the end of each row. If you're replacing a seat, tack some outdoor canvas to the underside of the chair for reinforcement. Use spray paint rather than a brush to paint the cane. Re-varnish with shellac in a spray bottle rather than enamel or polyurethane. One of the nicest things about cane furniture is its ability to flex and mould to the sitter. That's the squeaking sound you hear. Enamel and polyurethane weld the cane together as a solid block and you lose that comfort. They are also hard to remove if you decide you don't like the colour or if they get damaged. Shellac comes in a range of colours and is removable if you decide you don't like the colour.

METAL-FRAMED FURNITURE

Aluminium, chrome and stainless-steel furniture can be cleaned with vinegar and water on a cloth. If it's very dirty, use vinegar with bicarb. Clean wrought iron with bicarb and vinegar then wipe it either with baby oil or sewing machine oil. If it's painted, clean it with detergent and water. To create a high sheen and to prevent rust and corrosion, clean metals with car polish.

WOODEN FURNITURE

One of the great things about being a restorer is learning what all the expensive cleaning products are made of. I discovered that furniture polishes are based either on lemon peel and beeswax, orange peel and beeswax, canuba wax or silicone. Now you can make polish yourself! Be aware, though, that different wooden finishes require different kinds of cleaning.

Lacquer is made with layers of rice paper, plant resin, mineral dyes and vegetable gum and is difficult to keep in good condition. It should never be kept at less than 30 per cent humidity or it will dry out and crack. If it's in a dry spot, put a large bowl of water under it or place potted plants around it to create your own mini tropical climate. Use a damp cloth, never wet, to clean it. Never use detergents and see a specialist restorer for any significant problems. Small chips in black items can be covered with black boot polish.

Laminate can be cleaned with bicarb and vinegar.

Polyurethane can be cleaned with a damp cloth. For very dirty surfaces, use detergent. Keep water away from scratched surfaces. To repair any bubbling, inject with a syringe under each bubble a small quantity of 1 part *Unibond PVA* and 20 parts water. Put cling film over the bubble and weight it with a book or block. Leave for some time to allow it to dry.

Clean shellac with a good quality, silicone-free furniture polish or beeswax.

Varnish should be cleaned with a good quality, silicone-free furniture polish. If you have oily or grimy patches, scatter damp tea leaves over the stain and allow the tannins to break down and absorb the grime. Then polish with silicone-free furniture polish or beeswax.

Veneer should be cleaned with a good quality, silicone-free furniture polish applied with a soft cloth. Keep away from direct sunlight or the edges will lift.

If the wood on your new furniture is too shiny, wipe a mixture of talcum powder and cornflour over the surface with a piece of silk. If the wood is scratched and you would like to soften the mark, dampen the silk with vinegar first. Damp silk is more abrasive.

Problem:	**Scratches in wood.**
What to use:	**Baby oil; or coloured wax crayons, soft dry cloth.**
How to apply:	Baby oil is great for taking out small scratches and stains in woodwork. For larger scratches, use coloured crayons that are made of wax. Mix colours to match your wood and draw over the scratch. Then lightly polish with a soft dry cloth.

Problem:	**Scratches on polyurethane.**
What to use:	**Cornflour, silk bag, cloth; or *Brasso*.**
How to apply:	Put cornflour into a silk bag and dampen it so that

the cornflour works its way into the silk. This will act as a mild cutting agent. Rub the bag over the scratches then polish any residue off with a dry cloth. You can also polish with *Brasso*.

Problem: **Heat marks.**
What to use: **Beeswax, lemon peel; or bicarb, olive oil, cloth.**
How to apply: If the damage isn't too bad, use some warmed beeswax applied with the yellow side of the lemon peel (remove the flesh first). If it's quite damaged, use a mixture of 1 part bicarb and 1 part olive oil, paint it onto the mark, leave for a few minutes, then polish it off with a cloth before polishing normally.

Problem: **Small amount of woodworm in furniture.**
What to use: **WD-40; or old towels, paraffin, creosote, chemical resistant plastic, sawdust, fine sandpaper, Unibond PVA.**
How to apply: Place the skinny nozzle of the *WD-40* can on each hole and give a quick squirt. If there are more than ten holes, wrap the affected wood in old towels until the entire surface is covered, then pour a mixture of 10 parts paraffin and 1 part creosote over the towels. Wrap the area in chemical-resistant plastic and leave for 2–3 days. Be aware that this will remove any paint on the surface. Remove the plastic and towels, then finely sand back the wood. You may have to fill some of the holes created by the woodworm. The best way to do this is with sawdust. Finely sand a section of the wood on the underside or where it will not be seen. Then mix the sawdust with *Unibond PVA* to the consistency of stiff peanut butter and fill

the woodworm holes with it. Sand it smooth.

Problem:	**White stain on dark wood.**
What to use:	**Beeswax, turpentine, lemon peel or orange peel; or walnut juice; or toothpaste.**
How to apply:	The amount you need depends on how big the stain is. Warm 1 teaspoon of beeswax either in the microwave or by putting the tin in a small bowl of warm water. Mix it with 2–3 drops of turpentine. Then apply the mixture to the white stain with the outside or yellow part of a lemon peel. Take the inside of the lemon out first or the acid from the juice will bleach the wood. The oils and acids in the lemon are bleaching and moisturising agents. Orange peel works better with red cedar. Another technique involves cutting an unshelled walnut in half and rubbing the walnut over the white stain to darken it. One of the oldest ways to remove water rings from shellac is with toothpaste. Toothpaste is a mild abrasive and creates tiny holes over the water spot. When you wax it, the wax gets in behind where the stain was and fills up the air cavities.

Q: 'I hosted a dinner party the other night which went really well except candle wax dropped onto the dining table,' says Jane. 'How can I get it off without damaging the wood?'

Problem:	**Candle wax on wood.**
What to use:	**Ice, soft scraper, silk cloth, paper towel, hairdryer, rubber gloves.**
How to apply:	Harden the wax with ice, then remove as much as possible with a soft scraper. Make sure you scrape

along the grain of the timber. Rub the rest of the wax off with a damp silk cloth. Make sure it's real silk. If the wax has dripped onto unsealed wood, remove as much as possible with the silk cloth, then press a paper towel over the wax and heat with a hairdryer, keeping the paper towel over the wax as you dry. The wax will be absorbed by the paper towel. Keep changing the paper towel until the wax is completely removed. Wear rubber gloves so you don't get burnt fingers. Use a stop–start method so you don't overheat the wood and allow it to cool between each paper towel.

Q: 'I've got some wax on a French-polished table,' says Carole. 'Can I get it off without ruining the polish?'

Problem:	**Wax on polished wood.**
What to use:	**Warmed silk.**
How to apply:	You must use pure silk. Warm the silk first by wetting it and then placing it in the microwave. Then rub it over the wax. You can use a dry piece of silk but this will take longer to remove the wax.

Problem:	**Veneer lifting or bubbling.**
What to use:	**Syringe, *Unibond PVA*, water, cloths.**
How to apply:	Fill a syringe with 1 part *Unibond PVA* to 20 parts water. The mixture should be the consistency of runny cream. Inject a small quantity into the centre of the bubble or underneath the edge of the piece that is lifting, then press down. Place a weight, such as a heavy book, on it while it dries. (Use a piece of

cling film to protect the book.) To cover the injection hole mark, rub it with a hot damp cloth, leave it to dry and then polish with a dry cloth.

Q: 'I've got an old sewing machine with a wooden surface,' says Jan, 'but the veneer is cracking. Can it be fixed?'

Problem: Cracks in wood veneer.

What to use: Shellac, methylated spirits, cloth, 0000 steel wool; or *Unibond PVA* syringe, 0000 steel wool, methylated spirits, evenly bristled brush or sponge.

How to apply: If only the varnish is cracked, apply a new coat of shellac. For pre-mixed shellac, use 1 part methylated spirits to 4 parts shellac. If the shellac is not pre-mixed, mix shellac flakes and methylated spirits to the consistency of milk and apply with a cloth. The shellac will seep into the cracks and create a seal. It may need two or three coats. Allow each coat to dry for 24 hours before applying the next coat. Sand between coats with 0000 steel wool dipped in methylated spirits. If the surface is badly bubbled, use *Unibond PVA* and a syringe as described in 'Veneer lifting or bubbling' on page 78. Once it's dry, dip 0000 steel wool in methylated spirits and rub it along the grain. Then apply shellac with an evenly bristled brush or sponge along the grain. Allow to dry between coats.

Q:

'I'm restoring a pine chest of drawers,' says Martin. 'It's covered in shellac that is hard to get off. What do you suggest?'

Problem:	Removing shellac.
What to use:	Cotton or linen fabric, methylated spirits, cling film, 0000 steel wool.
How to apply:	Soak some cotton or linen fabric in methylated spirits so it's drenched. Lay it on the section of shellac you want to remove and leave for a while. The methylated spirits will break down the shellac and make it easier to remove. Methlyated spirits evaporates very quickly so place cling film over the fabric to slow the evaporation. Then scrub the shellac with 0000 steel wool dipped in methylated spirits. Alternatively, paint the drawers with methylated spirits and wrap them in cling film before scouring.

Problem:	Sticking drawers.
What to use:	Soap or candle wax; or spirit level, cardboard or block of wood, glue.
How to apply:	Rub the soap or candle wax along the runners. If this doesn't work, your chest of drawers may not be level. Check by using a spirit level, and if it's not even, put some cardboard or a block of wood under one of the legs. Also check that the joints of the drawer itself are secure. Re-glue them if they are loose.

CHINA/ORNAMENTS

These may be worth a lot of money, have sentimental value or simply be a decorating touch. A little attention is often the best approach with ornaments, particularly because dust can cause surfaces to craze. Whether they're clean or dirty, china pieces should be cleaned every six months. Keep a small container of water in display cabinets so the pieces don't dry out and never put your cabinet against an exterior wall because heat or cold will come through. A constant temperature is best for china. Dust with a hairdryer on a low setting and use a small paintbrush for difficult-to-reach areas. Secure items vulnerable to bumping by putting *Blu-Tack* underneath them.

Brass should be cleaned using a proprietary cleaner. If you're coating it, use shellac because it can be removed more easily. Be aware that brass will tarnish even after being coated but the coating will help it last a little longer.

Bronze should be cleaned with a damp soapy cloth but never rub bronze or you'll remove the patina.

Clay ornaments should be vacuumed and dusted regularly. Never soak because clay absorbs moisture. If you wash, do so quickly and dry thoroughly so you don't lift the glaze.

Cloisonné is enamel fused into small wire pockets on the outside of a bronze, brass or copper vessel. Clean it with vinegar and water. Never use soaps because it will tarnish.

Embroidery, where possible, should be kept out of direct sunlight. Keep it covered and inside cabinets. Hand wash gently if it's colour-fast. If not, take it to a restorer or good dry cleaner.

Ephemera should be kept as flat as possible under glass or in cabinets. Spray fabric with surface insecticide spray to keep bugs away.

Fabrics should be treated as you would your best table linen. Keep them well dusted and, where possible, vacuum.

Ivory can be cleaned with sweet almond oil applied with a cloth.

Lace should be hand washed in pure soap and rinsed very well. Glue medical gauze underneath a hole to hold it until you're ready to repair it properly. Embroider over the gauze in the same pattern as the lace and trim away any excess gauze.

Paper must be kept dust free and out of direct sunlight. Wash carefully with a slightly damp cloth. Just dab rather than wipe the paper. If in doubt, use a restorer or conservator.

Silver can be cleaned using a proprietary cleaner or bicarb and vinegar. Polish with bran.

Tinware can be wiped with warm soapy water and then dried thoroughly with a rag dampened with sewing machine oil. This will prevent rust. If tin does rust, apply *WD-40* with a cloth. To stop bugs eating paper labels on tinware, wipe the labels with a damp tea bag.

Wood can, if it's sealed, be cleaned using a good silicone-free furniture polish. If it's unsealed, clean with furniture oil.

Q: 'My daughter brought home some copper Buddha heads from Thailand,' says Katie. 'We sprayed them with a surface spray to get rid of any bugs, and black spots formed from the spray. Can we fix them?'

Problem:	Tarnished metal.
What to use:	Bicarb, vinegar, cloth.
How to apply:	Make a paste with 1 part bicarb and 1 part vinegar and apply it to the tarnish marks with a cloth. Don't get it on other surfaces or it will scratch. Allow the paste to dry then buff it off with a clean, dry cloth.

GLASS TABLETOPS

Clean glass with methylated spirits and a cloth. Then wipe the glass with a paper towel until it squeaks. Never use furniture polish on glass and see a restorer for scratches.

MARBLE TABLETOPS

Q: 'I've got water marks from leaving cups of tea on my marble-top table,' reveals Jocelyn. 'Can they be fixed?'

Problem:	Water marks in marble.
What to use:	Bicarb, vinegar, water, soft brush.
How to apply:	Sprinkle bicarb over the stain, then mix 1 part vinegar to 5 parts water and sprinkle it over the bicarb. When the mixture fizzes, rub with a soft brush.

TABLECLOTH STAINS

Q: 'I've got a policy of using my lovely things,' says Maria. 'We had a barbecue the other day and I used my white damask tablecloth. Now it's got sausage grease and tomato sauce over it. Can the stains be removed?'

Problem:	Grease and tomato stains on tablecloth.
What to use:	*Vanish*.
How to apply:	Tomato sauce fades in sunshine. You could also soak the stain in *Vanish*. The sausage grease will also come off with *Vanish*. If you're using good linen in vulnerable situations, buy some heavy-grade plastic from the hardware store and use a hairdryer to mould the plastic over the tablecloth. Be careful not to keep the hairdryer in one spot for too long or the plastic will melt.

Problem:	**Red-wine stain on tablecloth.**
What to use:	**Bicarb, sponge, white vinegar, cloth; or glycerine.**
How to apply:	For fresh stains, sprinkle some bicarb over the area then sponge with white vinegar. If the stain has set, rub bicarb in circles using a cloth dampened with vinegar. For any hard-set stains, soak in glycerine before removing the stain normally.

Q: 'One of my dinner guests misjudged the distance between the gravy boat and his plate,' says Carole. 'Now I've got a lovely brown stain on the tablecloth. What should I do?'

Problem:	**Gravy stain on tablecloth.**
What to use:	**Soap, cold water, hot water.**
How to apply:	Gravy contains proteins so you must remove them first with soap and cold water. Gravy also contains fat, which you remove with soap and hot water. Just make sure you clean with cold water first or you'll set the stain.

FIREPLACES

If your fireplace is operational, clean it after each use. To clean the surrounds, simply dust the area. To clean grime from anything except wooden surfaces, use vinegar.

Q: 'I've got smoke on the brickwork to the side of my fireplace,' says Jim. 'How can I get it off?'

Problem:	**Soot stains around the fireplace.**
What to use:	**Water, ash, cloths, bicarb, vinegar; or *Gumption*.**

How to apply: Add water to some powdered ash from the fireplace to create a slurry, or thin paste, and apply it to the stain with a cloth. Then wash with bicarb and vinegar. For light stains, combine ash with *Gumption* and wipe over with a cloth.

Problem: **Candle soot stains on the wall.**
What to use: **Vacuum cleaner, ash, sponges, soap, vinegar, water.**
How to apply: Candle soot is very greasy, so vacuum any loose particles then rub the soot with a small amount of ash on a dry sponge. Then wipe a little bit of soap onto the soot with another sponge. The soap picks up the last small pieces of soot. Finally, wipe down the surface with another sponge damped in vinegar and water.

HEATERS

Heaters are more efficient if they're dust free, clean and shiny. Clean and polish reflector plates at the back of the heater with bicarb and vinegar. This will also get rid of rust. Wipe the heating filaments with methylated spirits but don't turn the heater on until it's dried it out completely because methylated spirits is flammable.

   If you have a gas or kerosene heater and are irritated by the fumes, place a saucepan of water beside the heater as this will absorb them. Add a slice of onion to the water with kerosene heaters to help absorb the smells.

ENTERTAINMENT SYSTEMS

The main enemies of entertainment systems are dust, bugs and moisture.

Television screens, plasma screens and the exterior of most entertainment systems can be cleaned with 1 part methylated spirits to 4 parts water. Apply with a dust-or lint-free cloth, such as a T-shirt. Don't use detergent because it will leave smear marks. Vacuum all the vents at the back of the system using the brush head of the vacuum cleaner. Wipe the back of all electrics with a cloth sprayed with surface insecticide spray to keep insects away. When they're not in use, close all the doors and compartments of entertainment systems to stop dust getting in. Remove dust from difficult-to-reach areas with a camera puffer brush.

VCR heads should be cleaned using a high-quality video head cleaner or take them to a repairer. Store VHS tapes vertically like a book so you don't stretch the tape.

DVDs should be stored flat or they buckle. Wipe them with a DVD cleaner regularly. CDs should be cleaned using a CD cleaner and cloth if they are sticking.

Cassette players should have their rubber rollers and heads cleaned with a cotton bud dipped in methylated spirits.

Q:

'My girlfriend had a candle burning on top of the entertainment unit and wax dropped onto the fabric cover of the speaker on the TV. Can I get it out?' asks Mark.

Problem:	**Wax on fabric.**
What to use:	**Ice, plastic scraper, pins, tissues, hairdryer.**
How to apply:	If possible, take the speaker cover off. Then put ice on the wax and remove as much as possible with a plastic scraper. Next pin tissues to the waxy side of the speaker, turn the cover over and use a hairdryer on the back of the cover. This warms the wax up and the tissues absorb it. If you can't remove the

speaker cover, place a tissue over the wax and use the hairdryer to melt the wax from the front side. The tissue will then absorb most of it. Keep replacing the tissue until all the wax is absorbed. So you don't overheat the fabric, use a stop–start method.

OFFICE EQUIPMENT

This is another place where the enemies are dust, bugs and moisture. Vacuum often using the brush head attachment of the vacuum cleaner. Ventilate equipment well. If you have lots of cords around, tie them together with black bin bag ties so you don't get the spaghetti look.

Computers can be cleaned in a couple of ways. For light cleans, use a warm-water damp cloth. Never use a wet cloth because the ports can corrode. For dirty surfaces, apply some antistatic CD spray to a cloth and wipe it over all the surfaces, including the venting hole. Never spray directly onto the computer. Other specialised cleaners are also available. To deter bugs, spray surface insecticide spray on a rag and wipe the back of the computer with it. Keep computers ventilated by placing them at least 10 centimetres away from any wall.

The mouse should be cleaned when it becomes sticky and hard to move. To clean the inside, turn the mouse over and twist the back cover off the ball. Take the ball out and wipe it with a damp cloth. Never use chemicals on it. Then damp, but don't wet, a cotton bud with methylated spirits and clean the inside cavity of the mouse, including the rollers. When you've removed as much dirt as possible, carefully blow into the hole to make sure all the excess dust comes out. Put the ball back in and attach the back cover. To clean the underside of the mouse, dip a cotton bud in methylated spirits and wipe the slide points that make contact with the mat. Dry the mouse upside down. Give the mouse mat and the cord a wipe with methylated spirits to get rid of skin cell and sweat build-up.

Clean faxes with a warm-water damp cloth on the outside. Rubber rollers should be cleaned with methylated spirits on a cotton bud then wiped again with a water-dampened fluff-free cloth.

Telephones are best cleaned with glycerine on a cloth. Never use alcohol-based chemicals because they'll affect the plastic. And never use eucalyptus oil on plastics.

BOOKS AND BOOKSHELVES

Clean bookshelves once a week with a duster, or vacuum with the brush head. To stop books becoming mildewy, sprinkle silicone crystals along the back of the bookshelf or wipe the back of the bookshelf with oil of cloves.

Q: 'I've got cockroach droppings all over my books,' says George. 'How can I get rid of them?'

Problem:	Cockroach droppings on books.
What to use:	Vacuum cleaner, bicarb, old toothbrush; salt.
How to apply:	Vacuum first, then shut the book tight with the spine facing away from your hand. Sprinkle bicarb along the edges and rub with an old toothbrush. To prevent cockroaches returning, pile a bed of salt around the feet of the bookshelf.

Q: 'How can you get rid of awful smells in old books?' asks Graeme.

Problem:	Smelly books.
What to use:	Talcum powder.

How to apply: This is a very tedious process. Dust a page with talcum powder, then leave it in the sun for no more than three minutes or the UV rays will affect the paper. Clear the talcum powder, turn the page, apply more talcum powder, leave in the sun, remove the powder, and so on ... for the whole book!

 'I've got brown marks in my books,' says Sue. 'What should I do?'

Problem: Brown marks in books.
What to use: This is called foxing or book worm and is a job for a professional conservator.

WHITEBOARDS

 'I want to remove permanent pen from my white-board,' says Eric. 'What's your advice?'

Problem: Removing permanent pen from a whiteboard.
What to use: Perfume, cotton wool ball; or methylated spirits.
How to apply: Dab some perfume onto a cotton wool ball and wipe over the pen marks. If you don't have any perfume available, use methylated spirits applied with a cotton wool ball.

DECANTERS

I used to make wine at home and will never forget the day I mistook some *Dettol* for homemade brew. My throat had a menthol flavour for some time! It's best not to leave alcohol in your decanters for more than a day because it causes white cloudy smears or glass cancer.

Spirits should be stored in screw-top bottles and decanted just for the evening. Decanters are best washed in warm water and oven dried. To oven dry, turn your oven on to a very low heat then place the decanter in the oven, turn the oven off and leave. Never put direct heat, such as from a hairdryer, on a decanter as you risk cracking the crystal.

TRAYS

Trays are a great invention. Use silver cleaner to clean silver trays and a damp cloth to clean other trays.

'I've got a dull grey shadow on a silver tray,' reports Sue. 'Can I get rid of it?'

Problem:	**Shadow on silver tray.**
What to use:	**White toothpaste, silver polish, cloths.**
How to apply:	There are a couple of possible explanations for this. Some trays have nickel silver on the inside and electroplated silver coating on the outside. The silver coating may be wearing thin and exposing the core. Another explanation is that the tray may have been repaired with a different quality silver which is ageing at a different rate. To remove the shadow, wipe white toothpaste over it then clean with a good quality silver polish. Make sure you wash all the silver polish off and then polish with a dry cloth.

'What's the best way to clean a silver-plated tray?' asks Bill.

Problem:	**Cleaning silver-plated tray.**
What to use:	**Bicarb, vinegar, cloths; or bran, vinegar, cloths.**

How to apply: Sprinkle bicarb over the tray like icing sugar, then
splash vinegar over the top. Rub over the tray with a
damp cloth before polishing it with a dry cloth. You
can also mix bran and vinegar to form a paste and
rub it over the silver. Wipe off with a damp cloth
then a dry cloth.

ASHTRAYS

The best way to clean ashtrays is with cigarette ash. With a damp
cloth, rub ash over the ashtray and then wash in detergent and water.

Create your own air freshener

Mix ¹/₂ teaspoon of vanilla essence, cinnamon oil or eucalyptus oil
with a couple of drops of detergent into a spray bottle filled with
water. Or put some bicarb in a saucer with a couple of drops of
your favourite essential oil and mix well. This will absorb odours
and freshen the room. Never use eucalyptus oil if you're spraying
painted surfaces or plastic because it will strip them!

CLOCKS

Heirloom and antique clocks should be cleaned by a professional.
One of the best ways to maintain your mantle clock is to place an
oily cloth inside the sounding box. Use baby oil or sewing machine
oil. The dust and rust from the clock movements will fall to the cloth
and stick rather than flying around and damaging the workings of the
clock. The exterior should be cared for according to what it's made
of. Glass should be cleaned with methylated spirits. Never clean keys
with silver or brass cleaner. Just wipe them with an oily rag. No clock
should ever sit against the wall as air needs to circulate around it.
And always make sure clocks are level.

PIANOS

Most pianos are made of wood and are best cared for with a good
furniture polish. Piano keys can be made of plastic, ivory or ivorite. You
can tell which is which by the lines in the keys. Plastic keys have no lines.
Ivory has slightly uneven lines. Ivorite keys have even lines. Clean plastic
keys with glycerine. Ivory keys can be cleaned with sweet almond oil or, if
very dirty, with methylated spirits then sweet almond oil. If the keys are
really dirty, use a small quantity of toothpaste mixed with water and apply
carefully with a cotton bud. Then apply the sweet almond oil, which will
protect the ivory from cracking. Ivorite is cleaned with methylated spirits.

FLOWERS AND POT PLANTS

When I was younger, my job was to arrange flowers for the house.
We had fresh flowers in every room. Cut flowers will last longer if
you trim their stems just before putting them in water. They will also
last longer if you maintain the water level in the vase. Do this by
adding ice cubes to the vase every morning and night.

With daisies and soft-leaf plants, trim excess foliage and add a
pinch of salt and sugar to the water. This makes the flowers last
longer and stops the water from smelling.

To keep English violets longer, immerse the whole violet in water
for about two minutes and then place in a vase.

For roses, put a piece of copper in the water. Rescue wilting roses
by trimming the stems and filling the vase with chilled water up to
the bract or throat of the rose.

To prevent native flower stems going furry, put a small piece of
charcoal in the water. Proprietary products are available as well.

Remove the stamens from lilies before putting them in the vase
because they cause stains.

Artificial flowers

Plastic, fabric, silk and felt flowers can be dusted regularly with a
hairdryer on the cool setting. To clean paper flowers, hold them
upside down and lightly shake. Help retain their colour by keeping
them away from sunlight and deter bugs by placing two cloves in a
small green bag and attaching it to the stem. (Try to use a matching
green so the bag is camouflaged.)

THE ART OF DRYING FLOWERS: MERLE'S STORY

Incident: 'My daughter just got married and I'd like to dry her
wedding bouquet. It's made of coloured roses and
tulips.'

Solution: Remove all florist wire, plastic and ribbons. Then
place the bouquet upside down in a bowl slightly
bigger than the bouquet. Slowly add sand to the
bowl. As you do, vibrate the flowers so the sand gets
inside all the petals. Try not to bend or damage the
petals. When the bouquet is completely covered in
sand, put the bowl in the microwave for one-minute
bursts until the stems go woody. You can also use
the oven on the lowest possible temperature for
about three hours. A woody stem indicates that the
bouquet is ready. Then let the sand cool before
pouring it out. **Don't touch the sand while it's hot**.
Replace the wires and ribbons. Dried flowers can be
cleaned with a hairdryer on the cool setting. Keep
bugs away with a couple of cloves.

Vases

Vases can be tricky to clean, particularly the big narrow ones. If you're having difficulty removing dirt, cover the stain in baby oil and leave it for a couple of hours. Then remove the oil with either a paintbrush or a bamboo skewer with chewed ends. Make sure the ferrule, or metal part, is covered on the paintbrush so you don't scratch the vase. To access those hard-to-reach areas, create a curl in the end of a bamboo skewer and work it into the area.

Indoor plants

It's best not to keep indoor plants near radios, TVs or other electrical equipment. Plants don't like electromagnetic fields, and electrical equipment doesn't like water. An economical way to clean indoor plants that like water on their leaves is to stand them in the shower with a fine mist. Have a shower yourself as a small amount of soap keeps plants healthy.

Q: 'I've got ants making anthills in my pot plants,' says Cynthia. 'How can I get rid of them?'

Problem:	**Ants in pot plants.**
What to use:	*Borax*, **icing sugar or** *Nippon*.
How to apply:	Mix 1 part borax to 1 part icing sugar and create a mountain near the ants. Be careful because *Borax* is toxic. Wash the mixing spoon carefully after using it. Read the instructions before using *Nippon*. Wherever possible, find the source of the ants and pour boiling water on the nest rather than using poisons.

Floors, Walls and Windows

If you're not spilling stuff on your floors or walls then you're not living. Kids running around, friends over for coffee or a Sunday barbecue, pets traipsing muck over the house . . . This is the stuff of life and, like life, it's messy. Wine will be spilt, greasy sausages will be dropped and wax will drip. However, you can fix all these problems and never have to cry over spilt milk again.

JACKSON POLLOCK-STYLE CARPET: BEVERLEY'S STORY

Incident: 'I was cooking some chips in the oven and thought I'd been very clever putting some baking paper down first to collect the fat. After we'd eaten, I bunched the baking paper up and transported it to the bin. But I obviously didn't close off all the corners because when I turned around, I discovered a trail of oil drips right across my carpet. I've tried to clean it with bicarb, commercial cleaners, a hot iron and dry-cleaning fluid. Nothing has worked!'

Solution: Fill a bucket with cold water and enough detergent to generate a sudsy mix. Then apply the suds to the stain and scrub with an old toothbrush. Use as little water as possible. Then dry the spot with a paper towel or a chamois sponge block. Allow it to dry out and repeat the process until the stain has cleared. Detergent helps break down fats and brings them to the surface.

FLOORS

Floors are probably the most susceptible part of the house to dirt, spills and stains. One of my tricks if someone's about to visit and my hard floors are looking a bit dirty is to dampen an old T-shirt in water, wrap it around a broom head and run it over the floor. For regular cleaning, always vacuum or sweep before you mop.

Wood and cork

Before you throw your old tea leaves out, lightly scatter them over your sealed wooden floors! Yes, tea is a great way to clean them.

Just make sure the tea leaves are damp, not wet. Then vacuum them up immediately. It's a tip I learned from my grandmother who loved drinking tea as well. You can use tea bags instead by tying them behind your broom and then sweeping. After vacuuming, add a couple of drops of your favourite essential oil (I use lavender) to a bucket of water and wipe the floor with a mop. If you don't want to use tea leaves or bags, clean with 120 ml of vinegar per bucket of water. If the wood is unsealed, sprinkle bicarb then splash vinegar over the top. Scrub, then rinse with water.

To clean old urine stains on wood, use sugar soap. You may also need to repaint the wood or top up the varnish.

Problem:	**Squeaky floorboards.**
What to use:	**Talcum powder, wax.**
How to apply:	The squeakiness is usually caused by the boards rubbing together. Dust the floor with talcum powder, which will work its way between the boards and create a barrier. Then wax normally. I discovered this living in a house where all the floorboards were squeaky except the ones in the bathroom where talcum powder was scattered. I scattered talcum powder in the other rooms and they stopped squeaking. Great discovery!

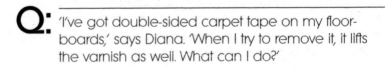

Q: 'I've got double-sided carpet tape on my floorboards,' says Diana. 'When I try to remove it, it lifts the varnish as well. What can I do?'

Problem:	**Adhesive on wood.**
What to use:	**Sticky tape, cloth, hot water, cling film, tea-tree oil, tissues.**
How to apply:	Remove as much of the adhesive gum as possible by

putting sticky tape over the top and quickly lifting it.
Do this several times. Then dampen a cloth in hot
water and lay it on top of the tape. Place cling film
over the top of the cloth and leave for 5 minutes.
Remove the cling film and the cloth and apply tea-
tree oil over the adhesive gum. Then roll the
adhesive gum off with tissues.

Tiles

One house I lived in had Spanish tiles with dark-coloured cement
grout. Every time I cleaned, the edge of the tiles used to smear with
dirt. That's because the previous owners never cleaned the grout
and it had collected layers of dirt and grime. I recommend using a
plastic scourer (not a steel one) for this task. Simply stand on it and
rub the scourer backwards and forwards over the grout.

To clean tiles, sprinkle with bicarb then splash vinegar and mop
the floor. Then rinse with hot water. The vinegar may cause the
room to smell a bit like a salad but this will dissipate and has the
added benefit of making the floor non-slip.

To seal terracotta tiles or unglazed Spanish quarry tiles, mix
1 part *Unibond PVA* to 20 parts water, mop it over the surface and
leave it to dry completely – between one and four hours, depending
on the weather. The seal will last for about three months.

Q: 'I've got a mop with a metal head and it's
darkened my tiles,' reports Bill. 'Is there a solution?'

Problem:	**Metal residue on tiles.**
What to use:	**Bicarb, vinegar, nylon brush, hot water, sticky tape.**
How to apply:	Sprinkle bicarb over the tiles, then splash with

vinegar and rub with a nylon brush. Rinse with hot
water. To prevent the problem, put sticky tape over
the metal.

Concrete

Q: Kerry's family had big plans to build their dream
home. 'We bought a block of land in a valley
and built a makeshift shed to live in while we
constructed the main house. Time went by and we
didn't end up building the house but decided to
stay in the shed and do it up instead. But we've
been living in it for eleven years and the concrete
slab has become really dirty. How can we clean
the slab before we put some tiles down?'

Problem:	**Dirty concrete floor.**
What to use:	**Bicarb, vinegar, stiff brush or stiff broom, mop.**
How to apply:	Sprinkle bicarb over the surface, splash vinegar over the bicarb, then scrub with a stiff brush or stiff broom. Rinse with warm water and a mop. If it's really dirty you may need to do this a few times.

Carpet

Buy the best quality carpet you can afford because the better the
quality, the less wear and tear you'll get. One of my sisters bought
cheap carpet and she had to replace it after five years. It's just not
worth it. Vacuum once a week, although this will vary depending on
the amount of traffic and dirt the carpet gets. I'd suggest using a
carpet cleaner every three months. After spraying the foam over the
carpet, scrub it with a broom head wrapped in an old clean white

T-shirt. Leave it to dry for about an hour, then vacuum. Doing this fairly regularly means your carpet never gets dirty enough to need a steam clean.

I like to clean woven carpet by scattering wheat bran across the top of it and scrubbing with a dry broom. Then vacuum. If the carpet is particularly grimy, damp bran with vinegar to form a clumpy, but not wet, mix and scatter it over the carpet. Then scrub with a broom before vacuuming.

To freshen up dingy carpets, make up a spray bottle containing 1 part bicarb to 3 parts vinegar and 5 parts water. Spray the carpet then sponge it, but don't go overboard and soak it. Sprinkling bicarb on the carpet before vacuuming is a good general carpet freshener, but won't necessarily clean stains. These will have to be spot cleaned.

Never put an iron on carpet. It will leave scorch marks on natural carpets and melt nylon or polyester ones. I discovered this when my ironing board broke and I put some sheets on the carpet to iron. The iron penetrated all those layers and left a nasty singe mark.

How to use the vacuum cleaner

I get a great sense of satisfaction from vacuuming. I love it. But to do it properly, you need to know about your machine. Did you know there are other attachments for the vacuum cleaner? Find them inside the cover of the vacuum cleaner or in a separate bag. These other brushes and nozzles will change the way you vacuum. It'll be as though you had one hand tied behind your back all that time. These are the components of the vacuum cleaner and what they do.

❑ Barrel: This is the main part of the cleaner. It has an inlet and outlet connection. The inlet is where the hose goes. The outlet is where the air blows out of the machine and it's generally covered. You can attach the hose here to backflush. A leaf blower is simply a reverse vacuum cleaner.

❑ Bag: Located inside the barrel. Modern vacuum cleaners have a window that shows when the bag is full. If you don't have this, check the bag each time you use the cleaner. It's a good idea to change the bag regularly. The vacuum cleaner won't work efficiently if the bag is more than half full.

❑ Tube (hard part): Vary the length of the hard part to suit your height or according to what you're vacuuming. Make it shorter when vacuuming furnishings and longer when vacuuming floors. If you are tall, extra lengths are available from the vacuum cleaner shop.

❑ Tube (soft part): The hose connection.

❑ Main head: This can be set to have bristles up or down. Put the bristles down for shiny and hard floors. Put the bristles up for soft floors, unless you have pets. Clean any fur out of the bristles with a comb.

❑ Brush head: This small round attachment with long bristles is designed to clean cobwebs and the surface of furnishings, curtains and pelmets.

❑ Corner nozzle: Use this to access tiny spaces such as the sides of chairs, to clean around the buttons on padded furniture, or to get right into corners on skirting boards or into the grooves of sliding door tracks.

Work from the top of the room to the bottom of the room. Begin vacuuming with the brush head and remove cobwebs from the ceiling. Then clean the tops of things such as wardrobes, picture rails, dado rails, skirting boards, light fittings, window frames and sills and so on. Then change to the corner nozzle. Go around the skirting boards and floors vacuuming corners and edges. Then attach the main head and clean under furniture first then the main areas. Start in one corner of the room and move diagonally across. Vacuuming diagonally puts less stress on the carpet fibres and leaves fewer marks. Just before you finish vacuuming, spray and suck up some insecticide into the cleaner to kill anything that might have landed in the bag. You could also put some oil of pennyroyal on a tissue and suck it into the bag – **but not if you are pregnant!**

If you're allergic to dust mites, suck a couple of damp tea bags into the vacuum cleaner bag before you start cleaning.

To find something small on the carpet, use your vacuum cleaner! Put a T-shirt between the head and the pole, vacuum the area and the item will stick to the T-shirt rather than going through to the bag. If you've dropped a packet of pins, needles or paper clips on the floor, attach a plastic magnetic strip across your broom or vacuum cleaner head with sticky tape. It'll pick them all up.

To clean the vacuum cleaner, vacuum inside the barrel and all the attachments, and clean the outside with a damp cloth. Wash the head in a mild detergent solution but make sure to dry it well so it doesn't rust.

Q: 'We have an elderly dog,' says Annie, 'and he's losing it a little bit. The other day he did a big poop in the hallway and walked it up and down the wool Berber carpet. What can we do?'

Problem: Pet mishaps on carpet/fabric.

What to use: Paper towel, bicarb, vinegar, sponge or nylon brush, vacuum cleaner; or bucket, cold water, detergent, old toothbrush, vinegar, water, bicarb, vacuum cleaner; or lavender oil, cotton wool ball, or camphor or mothballs; or bicarb, sponge, vinegar, nylon brush, vacuum cleaner or stiff brush; or ultraviolet light, chalk.

How to apply: Remove as much of the solids as possible then blot
with a paper towel until the carpet is touch dry.
Sprinkle a little bicarb over the spot then splash a
little vinegar. Scrub with a sponge or nylon brush and
leave to dry. Then vacuum it out and, if there's any
scent, do it again. Another way to fix the problem is
to fill a bucket with cold water and enough detergent
to generate a sudsy mix. Apply the detergent suds
with an old toothbrush, using as little water as
possible. Then fill a bucket with warm water and
detergent and apply the suds to the stain again with
an old toothbrush. The reason you use both cold and
warm water is because faeces contain proteins and
fats. Leave to dry. Get rid of any pet urine smell by
blotting with vinegar and water. Then sprinkle with
bicarb, allow it to dry and vacuum. Never soak urine
stains on carpet because this will just push the stain
further into the fibres.

Because animals like to return to the same spot,
put a small amount of lavender oil on a cotton wool
ball and lightly wipe it over the spot. This will deter
dogs. Use a combination of camphor and water to
deter cats unless you have coloured carpet, in which
case put some mothballs near the spot. Camphor can
bleach carpet.

For old pet stains, cover the spot with a large
amount of bicarb then wipe with a sponge dipped
in vinegar and scrub with a nylon brush. Dry
thoroughly. Then vacuum or sweep with a stiff
brush.

In the rather infuriating situation of being able to
smell but not locate an old stain, use an ultraviolet

(UV) light, not a black light. UV lights can be hired from a DIY shop. Under the light, the stains will fluoresce and glow. (Don't look into the ultraviolet light because it could damage your eyes and, unless you want a tan, don't stand in front of it.) Mark the stains with chalk. Then you've got the task of cleaning the stain up and a lot of bicarb and a little vinegar will come to your aid. Because the stains have been there for a while, you may have to repeat the treatment a few times.

Q:

'We've got some lilies sitting on a table in the lounge room,' says Mike, 'and the stamens have fallen off onto our white Berber carpet leaving a yellow stain. Can we get it out?'

Problem:	**Pollen stain on carpet/fabrics.**
What to use:	**Paraffin oil, cotton wool balls, methylated spirits, paper towel; plastic bag.**
How to apply:	If the stain has set, dampen it with paraffin oil applied with a cotton wool ball. Then damp the stain with methylated spirits applied with a cotton wool ball. Dry with a paper towel before repeating. Do this until the colour is removed. Some pollens will be easy to remove, others will need several attempts. To avoid the problem, I suggest you remove the stamens before putting your flowers on display. The best way to do this is by putting a plastic bag over your hand and pulling the stamens off into the plastic bag. Then wrap the bag over itself and throw it in the bin. That way your hands won't come into contact with the stamens.

Q:

'Our five-year-old was playing with nail polish and got a massive blob on the carpet,' reports Craig. 'Of course, it's right in the middle of the room. Is there a solution?'

Problem: Glue or nail polish stain on carpet.

What to use: Fine-toothed metal nit comb, tissue, cotton wool balls, acetone, hairdryer, cloth, methylated spirits; or superglue-removing liquids.

How to apply: This is a time-consuming and difficult task. Wrap a fine-toothed metal nit comb in a tissue so the teeth come through the tissue. Don't use a plastic comb because the acetone will melt it. Place the comb at an angle to the base of the carpet and wedge it underneath the stain. Dip a cotton wool ball in acetone and rub it over the top of the stain with the comb underneath. Work the stain row by row, using a clean cotton wool ball for each row. Acetone can affect carpet so make sure it doesn't penetrate the base. Replace the tissue if it's wet. This process is slow and may need to be repeated a few times. If it's an epoxy resin stain, warm it first with a hairdryer. Then dip a cloth in boiling water, wring it and lay it over the stain until the cloth starts to cool. Then pinch and pull the cloth to remove as much of the resin as possible. Repeat this a few times before using the acetone. To get rid of the smell of acetone, use methylated spirits and water. You can use acetone to remove superglue from carpet but it takes a long time. Try superglue-removing liquids for a quicker result.

Q:

'The other day, my son decided to help with the vacuuming,' says Rick, 'and he managed to suck up some lipstick which got stuck in the bristle of the cleaner head. Now there's lipstick all over the carpet. What can we do?'

Problem:	**Lipstick stain on carpet.**
What to use:	**Dry-cleaning fluid, cotton wool ball, bicarb, vacuum cleaner.**
How to apply:	Use dry-cleaning fluid applied with a cotton wool ball to soften the colour of the lipstick stain. Then sprinkle bicarb over the stain. Then vacuum.

Problem:	**Fruit stain on carpet.**
What to use:	**White cloth, vinegar, glycerine, cotton wool or old toothbrush, talcum powder, vacuum cleaner, carpet cleaner or *Vanish Oxi Action*, paper towel.**
How to apply:	Make sure the carpet is colour-fast*. For stains from fruits that go brown such as apricots, kiwi fruit, apples, bananas and so on, put glycerine on the stain with a cotton wool ball or old toothbrush and sprinkle talcum powder over the top of it. Vacuum. Then use a carpet cleaner. Vacuum again. An alternative to carpet cleaner is a paste of water and *Vanish Oxi Action* on the stain for a few minutes. Wipe it off, rinse and dry with a paper towel, leave the carpet to dry, then vacuum.

* To test for colour-fastness, soak a white cloth in vinegar and apply to part of the carpet not on display. If any colour comes off, it's not colour-fast and you may have to patch the carpet. How to do this is explained in 'How to patch carpet' on page 120.

Q:

'The kids spilled orange juice all over the carpet,' says Tina. 'How can I get it out?'

Problem:	**Orange juice stain on carpet.**
What to use:	**Carpet cleaner, cloth, lemon juice, ultraviolet light, cardboard.**
How to apply:	For fresh orange juice stains apply carpet cleaner. If the stain has set, wipe a cloth dipped in lemon juice over the stain before applying carpet cleaner. Then bleach it with sunlight. If you can't get the stain into the sun, hire an ultraviolet lamp. Protect the unstained part of the carpet with cardboard, cutting a hole around the stain. If you don't, the unstained carpet will bleach as well. Leave the lamp on the stain for up to 24 hours, checking every two hours. Don't look into the ultraviolet light because it could damage your eyes.

Q:

'I tried to get an orange juice spill out of the carpet with washing detergent and warm water,' reports Lynn, 'and now the stain has set and gone rusty. I need help!'

Problem:	**Orange juice stain set on carpet.**
What to use:	*Vanish Oxi Action*, **cloths, paper towels.**
How to apply:	Lynn's effort had the effect of setting the stain. Test in an unobtrusive spot to make sure this remedy won't leach the colour*. Unset the stain with a paste of water and *Vanish Oxi Action*, leaving it for a few minutes. Then remove the paste with a cloth and blot any moisture with a paper towel. You may have to repeat this process a couple of times. Be careful

not to get water on the carpet base or it will stain.
Have lots of paper towels at hand to absorb any
moisture immediately. Repeat if necessary.

    * If the carpet isn't colour-fast (check by soaking a
white cloth in vinegar and applying to a part of the
carpet not on display; if any colour comes off, it's not
colour-fast), you may have to patch the carpet. How
to do this is explained in 'How to patch carpet' on
page 120.

Q: 'One of the kids spilled lemonade on our dark-pink
carpet some time ago and we can't shift it,'
complains Michael. 'Do you have a suggestion?'

Problem:	Old lemonade/sugar stain on carpet.
What to use:	Glycerine, cotton wool ball, sponge or cloth, bicarb, nylon brush, clean white cloth, vinegar; or detergent, water, nylon brush, paper towel.
How to apply:	A sugar stain is very difficult to remove because it seeps right into the back of the carpet. For old stains, apply some glycerine to the stain with a cotton wool ball, and leave for a few minutes. Then wipe it off with a sponge or cloth. Sprinkle bicarb over the stain and scrub it in with a nylon brush. Then soak a clean white cloth in vinegar, wring it out and place it over the bicarb. Stand on the cloth so it absorbs the bicarb and stain. You may need to repeat this a few times. If the stain still doesn't shift, mix detergent and water to create a sudsy mix and scrub the suds into it with a nylon brush. Then place a paper towel over the spot to absorb the stain. You may need to repeat this a few times as well.

Problem: Furniture indentations on carpet.

What to use: Damp cloth, hairdryer, hairbrush, hairspray.

How to apply: Press a damp cloth over the spot. Then dry it with a
                  hairdryer, fluffing the carpet with a hairbrush as you
                  dry. If the carpet still lies flat, apply some hairspray
                  and dry it again with a hairdryer making sure to
                  backcomb.

Q: 'Our house was broken into,' says Robyn. 'The
police came and collected fingerprints, but they
left all this black powder on the carpet and I don't
know how to get it off. I rang the police and they
didn't know either!'

Problem: Black ink stain on carpet.

What to use: Milk, cloth, detergent, lemon juice; or dry-
                  cleaning fluid, cotton wool ball, talcum powder,
                  vacuum cleaner.

How to apply: The black powder is ink-based. Rot some milk in the
                  sun (the time it takes will vary) and rub the solids
                  into the stain with a cloth. Leave for a few minutes
                  then wash with a little detergent, lemon juice and
                  water. An alternative is dry-cleaning fluid applied
                  with a cotton wool ball. Then sprinkle some talcum
                  powder to absorb the dry-cleaning fluid. Vacuum.

Q: 'Our puppy chewed a red biro pen and got ink
all over our white carpet,' says Bob. 'What should
we do?'

Problem: Red ink on carpet.

What to use: Dry-cleaning fluid, cotton wool balls, vinegar.

How to apply: Red ink is particularly hard to remove. Apply dry-cleaning fluid to a cotton wool ball and rub it over the stain. Then apply vinegar to a cotton wool ball and rub it over the stain. Keep on doing this until the stain is removed.

Q: 'I dye my own hair,' says Chrissie. 'Usually I do it in the bathroom, but this time I was in the bedroom and I dropped some on the carpet. How do you get it out?'

Problem: Hair dye stain on carpet.
What to use: Hairspray, carpet cleaner; or dry-cleaning fluid, cotton wool balls.
How to apply: If you can get to the stain right away, use hairspray. Let it dry then treat with carpet cleaner. If you don't get to it immediately, put dry-cleaning fluid onto cotton wool and wipe it over the stain. Then wipe with clean cotton wool. Repeat until it's removed.

Q: 'I'm in big trouble,' admits John. 'I dropped a full plate of spaghetti bolognese on beige carpet and a white cotton sofa. It's a part of the house where eating usually isn't permitted. Can I be redeemed?'

Problem: Spaghetti bolognese stain on carpet/fabric.
What to use: Soap, sponge, ultraviolet light, cardboard.
How to apply: Because spaghetti bolognese contains protein, use cold water and soap with a sponge to remove the proteins first. Then use an ultraviolet light. Cover the non-stained area with cardboard to protect it and leave the light on the stain for up to 24 hours, checking it

every two hours. (Don't look into the ultraviolet light
because it could damage your eyes and, unless you
want a tan, don't stand in front of it.) You can do this
with the sofa too, but putting it in the sun is better.

Q:

'I was enjoying a beer on a very hot day but
spilled some on our white carpet,' says Ross. 'I did it
yesterday and the added complication is it's dark
beer. What should I do?'

Problem:	**Beer stain on carpet.**
What to use:	**Vinegar, paper towel, detergent, cold water, old toothbrush.**
How to apply:	Because the stain is a day old, damp it with vinegar and blot it with paper towel. You'll absorb even more of the stain if you roll the paper towel into a ball and stand on it. Then add detergent to cold water to generate a sudsy mix and spread the suds over the stain with an old toothbrush. Use as little water as possible. Let it dry and repeat the process until it's clean. For a new stain, remove as much of the beer as possible with a paper towel then mix detergent with cold water and apply the suds to the stain.

Problem:	*Blu-Tack* **stain on carpet.**
What to use:	**Ice, plastic bag, scissors, sticky tape, talcum powder, dry-cleaning fluid or tea-tree oil, cotton wool ball, tissue.**
How to apply:	Removing *Blu-Tack* from carpet is quite difficult. Place ice on the *Blu-Tack* first, either directly or inside a plastic bag. The *Blu-Tack* should become stiff and you can cut most of it off with scissors.

Don't cut the carpet fibres. Put sticky tape over the
Blu-Tack and rip it up several times. Then sprinkle
talcum powder over the remaining *Blu-Tack* and roll
it between your fingers. The powder will draw the
Blu-Tack out. For the remainder of the stain, use a
little dry-cleaning fluid or tea-tree oil on a cotton
wool ball and rub it in a circle. Then rub a tissue
over it and the *Blu-Tack* should stick to the tissue.

Q:

'I had some friends over to watch a DVD and one
of them dropped red wine on the carpet,' says
Steven. 'What's the best way to get it out?'

Problem:	**New red-wine stain on carpet.**
What to use:	**Bicarb, vacuum cleaner, vinegar, nylon brush.**
How to apply:	Cover the stain with a good amount of bicarb and let dry for a few minutes. Then vacuum and re-apply a smaller amount of bicarb, add a little vinegar and scrub with a nylon brush. Leave it to dry, then vacuum.

Problem:	**Old red-wine stain on carpet.**
What to use:	**Cloth, vinegar; or methylated spirits, cloth.**
How to apply:	Damp the stain with a cloth dipped in vinegar. If the stain doesn't come out, lightly damp it with methylated spirits on a cloth.

Problem:	**Boot polish stains and scuff marks on carpet.**
What to use:	**Eucalyptus oil, cotton wool; or dry-cleaning fluid.**
How to apply:	Rub eucalyptus oil over the spot with a cotton wool ball. An alternative is dry-cleaning fluid applied with a cotton wool ball.

Problem: Fat-based food stain on carpet.

What to use: Paper towel, hairdryer, bucket, detergent, old toothbrush; or dry-cleaning fluid, talcum powder, vacuum cleaner.

How to apply: Roll some paper towel into a ball, warm the carpet with a hairdryer then place the ball of paper towel over the stain. Stand on the paper towel so that as much of the fat as possible is absorbed. Fill a bucket with warm water and enough detergent to generate a sudsy mix. Apply the suds to the stain with an old toothbrush and scrub using as little water as possible. Place clean paper towel over the stain and stand on it. Leave to dry. Another option is to rub a small amount of dry-cleaning fluid into the fibres. Don't soak the carpet. Just damp it and lightly rub with paper towel. Cover with talcum powder to absorb the dry-cleaning fluid. Then vacuum the talcum powder.

Problem: Candle wax stain on carpet.

What to use: Ice, blunt knife, metal comb, paper towel, hairdryer.

How to apply: Put ice on the wax to harden it then scrape as much away as possible with a blunt knife. Wedge a metal comb underneath the wax and put a paper towel on top of the wax. Then use a hairdryer over it. The paper towel will absorb the wax. Repeat until all the wax is removed. Never use an iron on carpet as it can char natural fibres or melt synthetic fibres.

Q: 'My two-year-old wanted to help me bring the shopping in,' reports Megan. 'So I gave her a carton of cream which she dropped on a green rug. It's created a white shadow and really smells. What can I do?'

Problem:	Cream stain on rug/carpet.
What to use:	Detergent, old toothbrush, paper towel; or dry-cleaning fluid, cotton wool ball, talcum powder, vacuum cleaner, carpet cleaner.
How to apply:	Attack the proteins first. Mix enough detergent in cold water to generate a sudsy mix and apply just the suds to the stain with an old toothbrush. Then dry with paper towel. Remove the fats with detergent suds mixed in hot water. Apply the suds only to the stain with an old toothbrush, then dry with a paper towel. An alternative is dry-cleaning fluid applied with a cotton wool ball. Sprinkle talcum powder over the dry-cleaning fluid to absorb it. Then vacuum. To get rid of the smell, use carpet cleaner.

Problem:	Old coffee and tea stains on carpet
What to use:	Glycerine, cotton wool ball, sponge, white vinegar, bicarb, vacuum cleaner.
How to apply:	Apply glycerine to the stain with a cotton wool ball. Leave for 5 minutes then damp sponge the stain with white vinegar. Sprinkle with bicarb then vacuum when dry.

Q: 'What can you do about old vomit stains in the carpet?' asks Maryann.

floors walls windows spotless

Problem: Old vomit stains on carpet.

What to use: Glycerine, cotton wool ball, milk, cloth, vacuum cleaner, cloth, carpet cleaner.

How to apply: How to clean vomit will depend on what's in it. Because the stain has been there for some time, apply glycerine with a cotton wool ball to the stain. Then rot some milk in the sun (the time it takes will vary) and apply the solids to the stain with a cloth. Leave until almost dry, vacuum and then wash the solids out with a damp cloth. Then clean the area with carpet cleaner.

Q: 'My wife opened a tube of foundation make-up and dropped it all over our white wool carpet,' reports Brian. 'Is there a way to get it out?'

Problem: Make-up on carpet.

What to use: Detergent, old toothbrush, paper towel, carpet cleaner; or lemon juice or ultraviolet light, cardboard.

How to apply: Work out if the make-up has oil in it first. If it contains oil, clean that out by mixing detergent in cold water and applying just the suds to the stain with an old toothbrush. Dry with a paper towel. Then clean the area with carpet cleaner. Sunlight will bleach the stain. If you can't get the carpet into the sun, apply some lemon juice to the stain or hire an ultraviolet light. Protect the unstained part of the carpet by covering it with cardboard or it will bleach as well. Leave the ultraviolet light on the stain for up to 24 hours, checking it every two hours. Don't look into the ultraviolet light because it could damage your eyes.

Q: 'I've got some ingrained chewing gum in my carpet,' says Mary. 'I'd love to get rid of the awful stuff. What do you suggest?'

Problem:	Chewing gum on carpet.
What to use:	Ice, knife or scissors or ice-cream stick, cotton bud, dry-cleaning fluid, eucalyptus oil or tea-tree oil, tissues, vacuum cleaner.
How to apply:	Put ice on the chewing gum to harden it. Then cut out the hardened gum with a knife, scissors or an ice cream stick. Once you've removed as much chewing gum as you can, dip a cotton bud in dry-cleaning fluid and slowly work over the chewing gum. Then apply eucalyptus oil or tea-tree oil to the gum and rub the area in circles with a tissue. Then vacuum.

Problem:	Singe/burn on carpet.
What to use:	White cloth, vinegar, 3 per cent hydrogen peroxide, damp cloth, scissors.
How to apply:	Test the carpet for colour-fastness first. Do this by soaking a white cloth in vinegar and applying it to a part of the carpet not on display. If any colour comes off, it's not colour-fast. If it is colour-fast, cut a cloth to the size of the burn and dip it in 3 per cent hydrogen peroxide. Then lay it over the mark for two minutes. Rinse with a damp cloth. If the burn is very bad or the carpet isn't colour-fast, clip the surface of the wool with scissors or patch it. How to do this is explained in 'How to patch carpet' on page 120.

Q: 'It's a rather sad story,' warns Bronwyn. 'My husband and I went away for the weekend and left the three teenage boys at home. The dog had an accident on the carpet and one of the boys cleaned it with the first thing he found in the cupboard, which was tile cleaner. He sprayed it on the carpet and now there's half an acre of brown on the carpet. What can I do?'

Problem: Tile cleaner sprayed on carpet.
What to do: Patch the carpet.

How to patch carpet

Cut around damaged part of the carpet into a manageable shape with a Stanley knife. Find a piece of the carpet (perhaps some leftover or cut from somewhere little seen, such as from inside a cupboard) a little larger than the stained area. Make sure the pattern is in the same direction. Then make a paper template of the stained area and transfer this to the piece of patch carpet. Cut the patch carpet around the template with a sharp knife. You'll need some carpet tape, which is available from carpet manufacturers, dealers and hardware shops. Attach the tape under the edges of the damaged carpet so that the adhesive side is facing upwards. Make sure that half of the tape is under the old carpet and the other half is exposed in the hole. Then press the patch carpet into the hole, sticking it to the exposed half of the tape. Brush the carpet in both directions until the fibres line up on the edges. Stand on the area for five minutes to make sure it sticks well. Then place a book on top of the patch for 24 hours.

Rugs and mats

Rugs are handy for high-traffic areas and if you have children. The less dirt a rug or mat accumulates, the longer it will last. And, unlike carpet, you can take it outside and give it a good whack.

To take care of an Oriental rug, give it a vacuum, then wrap a hair brush in an old T-shirt that's been soaked in a small amount of hair conditioner and warm water. Brush the rug with this until it's damp but not wet. This will keep the fibres soft. Once you've finished, use the hairbrush again, without the T-shirt, to fluff the fibres up. Then vacuum again. The number of times you'll need to do this will depend on how much traffic the rug gets. If it has a lot of feet tramping over it, do this every two months. Your rugs are less likely to absorb stains if you Scotchguard them after cleaning.

Problem:	**Rug/mat edge is lifting.**
What to use:	**Rubber mesh or wire claw.**
How to apply:	One option is to place a rubber mesh on the back of the rug or mat. Another option is to attach a wire claw to the edge of the rug to help keep it flat. Both are available from carpet manufacturers.

Sisal

Sisal is best cleaned by sweeping. Never use wet cleaners on it. I find the best cleaning method is mixing bran and vinegar until clumpy but not wet. Scatter it over the sisal and sweep backwards and forwards, then vacuum. Bran acts as a scourer and absorbent.

Coir

This type of flooring attracts insects so vacuum regularly. To deter bugs, soak a tissue in oil of pennyroyal **(do not use if pregnant!)** and suck it into the vacuum cleaner before cleaning. You can also leave mint bags in the corner of the room to deter bugs. Use a mixture of wheat bran and vinegar to clean as described with sisal.

Linoleum, vinyl and self-levelling plastics

Linoleum, or lino, is formed by coating hessian or canvas with linseed oil. Developments with plastics mean there are now numerous variations on the lino theme. Clean by sprinkling bicarb over the surface, then splashing vinegar on top and mopping. Then rinse with hot water and leave to dry.

Q: 'I've got large marks from a ballpoint pen on my lino floor,' reports Julie. 'How do I get it off?'

Problem:	Ink/ballpoint pen stain on linoleum.
What to use:	Cotton bud, dry-cleaning fluid; or milk, old toothbrush; or kerosene, cotton wool ball.
How to apply:	Dip a cotton bud in dry-cleaning fluid and wipe it over the biro marks. You could also rot some milk in the sun. Scrub the solids into the stain with an old toothbrush, then wash out. If the ink is red, and the flooring is lino, apply kerosene with a cotton wool ball. Those with vinyl or self-levelling plastics will have to live with the red. It's impossible to move!

DOORS

One of my tricks if the house is a bit untidy and visitors are about to arrive is to wipe the doorjambs with lavender oil. The smell creates an impression of cleanliness and also keeps insects away! Clean doors every couple of months or when they become grubby. If the door has a high polish or laminate finish, clean with detergent and water. If it has a French polish finish, use a good quality, non-silicone furniture polish. Wipe greasy hand marks with a damp cloth. Door handles made of chrome, brass or glass should be cleaned with bicarb and vinegar on one sponge.

If your door squeaks, rub the hinges with soap. If the door lock is jammed or stiff, use a graphite puffer either into the hole of the lock or in the slots around the edge of the lock tongue. If the door is sticking and you can't work out where to sand it, rub chalk down the doorframe, shut the door and the chalk will transfer to the part of the jamb that needs sanding.

How to fix a key broken in a lock

Have you ever broken a key in a lock? To repair it yourself, you need some superglue—which is hopefully on the same side of the locked door as you are! Put a very small amount of superglue on the broken edge of the key in your hand and line it up very carefully with the broken edge in the lock. Do not get glue on the lock itself. Connect the head and shaft of the key and hold it carefully for 3 minutes. Then gradually ease the broken piece out. Avoid twisting the key when pulling it out. Make sure you have a replacement key cut.

LAMPS AND LIGHT SHADES

Lamps illuminate a room and are generally responsible for creating the mood as well. It's a big ask! Light shades made of fabric should be dry cleaned or cleaned with carpet cleaner. Once the carpet cleaner has dried, use the brush head on your vacuum cleaner to remove it. Make sure the brush is clean first or you'll create more mess. Glass light shades should be cleaned in warm water. Clean brass and metal arms with a good quality brass polish. And make sure you don't get cleaning product in the electrical fittings. To cut down on bugs, spray the tops of light shades with surface insecticide spray.

Every time you change a light bulb, clean the other light bulbs with a cloth and they'll shine brighter. To prevent halogen lights corroding, wipe the connection on the bulb with a cloth once a week.

Problem:	**Broken light bulb in light socket.**
What to use:	**Rubber gloves, carrot.**
How to apply:	Make sure the light is off and that you're wearing some rubber gloves. Get a carrot, cut the top off and jam the carrot base into the light bulb socket. Then twist or turn and remove. Make sure you remove any small pieces of broken glass before putting in a new light bulb.

Cleaning chandeliers

They're beautiful and decadent and difficult to clean. However, the task of cleaning is made a little easier with the product Crystal Clear. Turn the light off at the switch and put a sheet or towel underneath the chandelier of a size suitable to cover the entire drip line. Using a ladder so you can reach the chandelier comfortably, remove the light bulbs and put a small plastic bag over each of the fittings so you don't get moisture in the electrics. Dust the tops of the chandelier with a soft brush then spray a generous amount of Crystal Clear until the chandelier is damp and starting to drip. The dirt and dust will run off. If it's been a while since you last cleaned it, you may need to apply Crystal Clear again. When the chandelier is completely dry, clean and return the light bulbs.

WALLS

It's inevitable that you'll get marks on the walls, especially in high-traffic areas or if you have little people with grubby hands who use the wall as a convenient support. Be careful using commercial products to clean marks because most have an alcohol base that can break down the paint surface and leave a bleached shiny spot. Clean your walls every couple of weeks either with a broom or vacuum cleaner. Put an old T-shirt over the top of the broom or vacuum to prevent bristle marks. Some dirty marks will come off with a good pencil eraser. You could also try rolling brown bread into a ball and rubbing it against the wall. If these don't work, try a very diluted solution of sugar soap applied with a soft cloth. Wring the cloth tightly before applying. For build-up around switches, apply vinegar and water sparingly with a sponge. To avoid drip lines, start cleaning from the bottom and work your way up, drying as you go. To prevent spider webs on the ceiling and wall edges, put a small drop of lemon oil on your cobweb brush. Spiders don't like lemons.

Problem:	**Crayon marks on the wall.**
What to use:	**Cotton wool ball, dry-cleaning fluid, soft brush, clean cloth.**
How to apply:	Damp the cotton wool in dry-cleaning fluid and wipe over the mark. Then brush the mark gently with a soft brush. Blot the rest with a clean cloth. Always work from the outside to the inside of the mark.

Problem: **Mould on the wall.**

What to use: **Oil of cloves, bucket, soft cloth or sponge.**

How to apply: Put 4–5 drops of oil of cloves in a bucket half filled with water. Wipe this over the mouldy wall with a soft cloth or sponge. The mould may not come off all at once but the oil of cloves will continue to kill it. Dust the mould off later.

Problem: **Double-sided tape on the wall.**

What to use: **Detergent, clean fabric, cling film; or hairdryer, cloth, dry-cleaning fluid, cotton bud.**

How to apply: Add a little detergent to boiling water, wet some clean fabric in it, wring it out and place it over the tape. Then put cling film over the top of the fabric and leave until the heat penetrates the glue. You should be able to lift the edge of the tape with your fingers when it's ready. Never use a knife because you can tear the paint on the wall. Alternatively, heat the adhesive with a hairdryer, then rub a piece of cloth over it and peel away. The remaining adhesive can be removed with dry-cleaning fluid on a cotton bud.

Wallpaper

You may be a sandwich short at lunch because of this. A slice of fresh bread rubbed over wallpaper is a great way to clean it. The kind of bread you use will depend on the colour of the wallpaper. Brown bread is more abrasive but may transfer colour to light walls.

Q: 'I've got three boys under the age of ten and, one day, they decided to plaster the wallpaper with peanut butter, jam and margarine,' says Jane. 'It's a disaster!'

Problem:	**Peanut butter, jam, margarine on wallpaper.**
What to use:	**Detergent, paper towel, damp cloth.**
How to apply:	Do not use water. Put detergent onto a paper towel and wipe it over the wallpaper. The detergent will break down the fats in the food. You'll need to do this several times. Then wipe with a damp cloth.

PICTURES, PAINTINGS AND MIRRORS

Look after your paintings just in case the one you inherited from Uncle Harry is worth a fortune. Even if you don't have a hidden treasure, care should still be taken looking after them.

Acrylic paintings can be cleaned with a damp cloth.

To remove residue and dust from oil paintings, clean with stale urine, salt and potato. Yes, you did read stale urine! Collect 1 litre of female urine and leave it in the sun for a week. It will reduce to ½ litre. Then add 1 tablespoon of salt and 2 tablespoons of raw grated potato to it. Allow the mixture to sit for half an hour. Dampen a cloth in the mixture, wring it and then wipe over the painting. Then damp a clean cloth in water and wipe the painting gently. Pat it dry. You can also rub brown bread over the painting to clean it. For any serious cleaning problems, see a restorer.

Water colours should be cleaned by a professional.

Never use alcohol-based cleaners such as methylated spirits or turpentine on gilded frames. Most gilding is covered with a layer of shellac and alcohol-based cleaners will compromise it. Instead, dust the frame with a hairdryer on the cool setting. This should be enough to clean it, but if dirt remains, wipe a damp cloth over the frame and then dry it with a soft cloth.

Clean glass with methylated spirits and a cloth. But be careful not to get methylated spirits around the edges or it could seep into the print. Polycarbonate should only be cleaned with a damp cloth. Clean metal and wood as you would furniture. Clean plastic with glycerine.

Protect paintings by spraying a cloth with surface insecticide spray and wiping it over the back of picture frames. Don't touch the painting, just the frames.

Mirrors can be cleaned with methylated spirits but be careful of edges, particularly with gilded frames. Rather than buying a new mirror, which can be very expensive, find a lovely old second-hand frame and see a glazier who will supply, cut and fit a mirror to size very cheaply.

Problem:	**Flaked or chipped gilding.**
What to use:	**Soft cloth, Gilder's Size and Gilder's Gold Dust.**
How to apply:	Clear any dust with a soft cloth then paint the bare section with a thin coat of Gilder's Size. Allow it to dry until it's tacky then dust with Gilder's Gold Dust, which is very fine gold dust. Brush off any excess.

WINDOWS

The best way to clean glass windows is with methylated spirits and water in a spray pack. Spray the solution on the window then polish the glass with a paper towel. When cleaning windows, always use vertical stripes on the outside and horizontal stripes on the inside. That way you can tell which side a smudge is on. The vertical stripes should be on the outside because that's the way rain falls, and any horizontal lines catch moisture and dust and leave grimy lines.Vertical lines allow the dirt to run away, leaving windows looking cleaner for longer. Don't use newspaper to clean windows. They used to be good when the ink contained lamp black, but today's newspapers use rubber-based ink, which leaves a smear. Use paper towels instead.

Window frames and sills

Every time you vacuum the floor, vacuum the windowsills as well. Then wipe them with a mixture of 240 ml of vinegar to 1 bucket of water. Keep putty in good condition by wiping a small amount of linseed oil over it twice a year if the putty is unpainted. If the putty is painted, make sure it's painted all the way to the glass otherwise the putty will allow oil to smear out over the glass. To help prevent rubber seals perishing, wipe them with vinegar and water. Never poke at silicone because if you break the seal it becomes exposed and mildew can grow. Clean it with water.

Clean marble windowsills with bicarb and 1 part vinegar to 5 parts water. Then polish with cera wax. To inhibit mildew, add 1 drop of oil of cloves to half a cup of cera wax.

For sandstone windowsills, clean with bicarb and vinegar. Inhibit mildew by adding oil of cloves to hot rinse water.

Clean painted wooden windowsills with vinegar and water. If they're varnished, clean with a good quality, non-silicone furniture polish. Wipe unsealed cedar with a good quality furniture oil which will continue to feed the wood. If it's gone grey, wipe it with a wet tea bag, then allow it to dry before oiling it.

Rubbing a cake of soap along the window frame and sashes will allow the window to move more smoothly.

Curtains

Someone living on a busy road will have to clean their curtains more often than someone living in a sleepy hollow. Hand wash or dry clean curtains according to the instructions. After washing coloured curtains, hang them upside down so the colour doesn't run. Don't dry them in direct sunlight or they'll bleach.

To clean chintz and cretonne curtains, place 115 g of bran in a saucepan with 1 litre of water and slowly bring it to the boil. Let it simmer for a few minutes and then strain it. Combine the strained liquid with an equal amount of lukewarm water. Dip the curtains and then hang them straight. This will clean and stiffen the fabric. If you need to replace the sheen on chintz or cretonne, use a combination of 1 part glycerine, 1 part egg white and 20 parts water in a spray pack. Spray it on the front surface of the fabric then use a warm iron. Don't use this on muslin, net or fine lace.

Velvet curtains should be cleaned with bran in either a muslin or silk bag. Rub the bag over the tufts.

When ironing curtains, always iron top to bottom. This will keep the top edges straight and the curtains will hang better. If you don't want to iron the curtains rehang them slightly damp and allow them to dry in fresh air. Just make sure the windows are clean or you'll have dirty curtains again.

Problem:	**Yellowed nylon net curtains.**
What to use:	**Washing powder, methylated spirits.**
How to apply:	Wash the curtains with washing powder in the washing machine and add 120 ml of methylated spirits to the rinse cycle. Then hang out on the line until they're almost dry before hanging them back on the rod to fully dry. Never put nylon in the dryer.

Q: 'My cat sprayed on my new curtains,' says Chris. 'The smell is awful and there's a slight stain.'

Problem:	**Cat spray on curtains.**
What to use:	*Vanish*, lavender oil, spray pack, camphor flakes.

How to apply: To remove the stain, wash the curtains in a bucket with *Vanish* (for quantity, follow directions) and water. Add a few drops of lavender oil to the water to get rid of the smell. Rinse and hang on the line. If the smell remains, add a couple of drops of lavender oil to water in a spray pack and spray over the area. Leave some camphor flakes nearby to deter the cat.

Venetian blinds

Don't throw your old kitchen tongs out. They can be recycled and reinvented as venetian blind cleaners. Glue some sponge to both inside edges of the tongs and leave to set. Then place the tongs over the top and bottom of each blind, pinch the tongs together and run them along. The sponge can be wet or dry. To clean the cords, use a mixture of vinegar and water and apply with a sponge. Start from the top and wipe down so the liquid soaks into the cord. The second time you do this, squeeze the moisture from the cord. You may have to do this a few times to remove all the dirt.

To thoroughly clean venetian blinds, take them down and lie them outside. Fill a bucket with a mild detergent solution and then, with a broom, wash the venetians backwards and forwards, shutting one side and then the other. Hang them on the clothesline and wash them down with a hose. Leave to dry.

Wooden blinds and plantation shutters

Wooden blinds and shutters can be dusted in the same way as venetian blinds – with those old tongs! You can also clean them by putting on some white gloves and running your fingers along the top and bottom of the slats. The only problem is your fingers may become sore if there are a lot of blinds to clean.

How to apply: Mix 1 teaspoon of oil of cloves and 2 teaspoons of oil
of pennyroyal with 2 litres of warm water in a spray
pack. Go into the roof of the house and spray the
mixture on the stains. Then sprinkle bicarb over the
stain to absorb the urine. You may need to repaint
the ceiling if the stain has penetrated. **Do not use
pennyroyal if you are pregnant.**

Q: 'I can't stand the smell of naphthalene flakes,'
reports Rebecca. 'I've put the flakes around to
deter a rat at my place. Is there any way to get rid
of the smell?'

Problem: Smell of naphthalene flakes.
What to use: Lemon thyme.
How to apply: Sprinkle some lemon thyme wherever the
naphthalene was placed. The better way to deter rats
is with with snake poo, as explained below!

Getting rid of mice

When I lived in the country, some mice took up residence in my
house. After a while, I noticed they'd disappeared. A few months
later, I saw a massive snake sliding from the ceiling, thankfully
outside the house. Its length was the height of the building. Then
the mice came back. I mentioned this to a neighbour who told
me snakes deter mice. So the solution for mice is either to have a
snake in the house or, more pleasantly, scatter some snake poo
inside the ceiling or under the house. The poo is a small pellet,
doesn't smell and should last for about twelve months. Ask your
local pet shop for some.

The Bedroom

We spend a third of our lives in the bedroom. Sure, most of it is spent sleeping, but when you're awake, it's your room. It's a sanctuary. How can you make your bed a joy to slumber in? And what can you do if breakfast in bed becomes breakfast all over the bed? Read on and all will be revealed.

The bedroom is also where we keep our clothes. Care for them now and you'll still be able to wear them years later when they come back into fashion.

NEVER PAINT YOUR TOENAILS IN BED: SUE'S STORY

Incident: 'It was so stupid! I was painting my toenails in bed
                  and dropped some polish on the sheets. And of
                  course it's the brightest red nail polish you can
                  imagine. And they're my favourite sheets—lovely
                  Egyptian cotton. Is there anything I can do?'

Solution: Put a cotton wool ball behind the stain then soak
                  another in acetone (not nail polish remover) and rub
                  it in a circular motion on the front of the stain. Use
                  the dry cotton wool ball as backing. Work from the
                  outside to the inside of the stain. Keep on doing this
                  until all the colour is removed, replacing the cotton
                  wool balls as you go. With some nail polish, this
                  process will need to be repeated up to five times.

BED

The importance of a clean and comfortable mattress becomes really
evident when you don't have one. Just ask any backpacker,
especially one scratching bedbug bites! I like to air, turn and vacuum
mattresses often. If you can, let yours air for about 15 minutes every
day before making the bed. And get into the habit of turning the
mattress over and backwards, each week if possible. This may
sound excessive but it keeps the coils even and stops the mattress
from sagging. To help you remember where you are in the rotation
cycle, attach a different coloured safety pin to each corner. I'd also
recommend a monthly sprinkle of bicarb over the mattress; leave it
for a couple of hours and then vacuum it off.

An indispensable part of any bedding is a mattress protector. It's
a great washable barrier between you and the mattress and allows
air to circulate. Wash it according to the instructions every third

time you change your sheets. If you have a headboard, vacuum it once a week.

If you spill something on the mattress, use as little moisture as possible to clear it off. It's better to apply a little bit of solvent a few times than use too much at one time. Use a hairdryer to speed up the drying time.

How to kill dust mites

I suffer from asthma and use this remedy to kill dust mites. Put a tea bag into a spray bottle filled with cold water; let it sit for 3 minutes and then lightly spray the liquid over the mattress. The tannins in the tea kill mites. And no matter how clean you are, you can get bedbugs, which live wherever people do. Keep them contained with tea-tree oil. Rub some onto your fingers and then wipe around the edge of the mattress. Use surface insecticide spray over the edges and ends of the bed, but not over the top of the mattress and not just before you're about to sleep in the bed.

Q: 'On weekends, I love having a cup of tea in bed,' confesses Leanne. 'But one morning, I lost control of the cup and now the mattress is covered in tea. What can I do?'

Problem:	**Tea stain on mattress.**
What to use:	**Glycerine, cotton wool, detergent, cloth, hairdryer.**
How to apply:	Apply glycerine with a cotton wool ball. Use enough to make the surface of the mattress damp but not soaked. Leave for 10–15 minutes then wash it off with a little detergent on a damp cloth. Leave to dry or speed dry with a hairdryer. Never hand a sleepy person a cup of tea in bed because it's likely to end up all over the mattress. It's happened to me!

Problem: Coffee stain on mattress.

What to use: Glycerine, cotton wool, detergent, cloth, hairdryer.

How to apply: Apply glycerine with a cotton wool ball. Use enough to make the surface of the mattress damp but not soaked. Leave for 10–15 minutes then wash it off with a little detergent on a damp cloth. Leave to dry or speed dry with a hairdryer.

Problem: Fresh bloodstain on mattress.

What to use: Bar of soap, cloth.

How to apply: Moisten the bar of soap with cold water and rub it on the stain, working from the outside to the inside of the stain. Rinse several times with a cloth wrung out in cold water. Leave it to dry and repeat if needed.

Problem: Old bloodstain on mattress.

What to use: Cornflour, cloth, stiff brush.

How to apply: Make a paste of cornflour and water to the consistency of thickened cream. Paint it on the stain with a cloth and leave to dry. Brush the dried mixture off with a stiff brush. You may need to do this a few times.

Q: 'I write a lot in bed,' says David. 'But I had a disaster when my ballpoint pen broke and ink went everywhere, including into the mattress. What should I do?'

Problem: Ink/ballpoint pen stain on the mattress.

What to use: Milk, detergent, cloth; or dry-cleaning fluid, cotton wool ball, detergent, sponge, paper towel, hairdryer, talcum powder, vacuum cleaner.

How to apply: Rot some milk in the sun (the time it takes will vary). Then place the milk solids on the stain, and with your hand, gently rub the solids in a circle over the stain. As the area dries, you will see the ink start to rise up through the milk solids. Remove the solids with some detergent suds on a cloth, using as little water as possible. An alternative to rotten milk is dry-cleaning fluid applied with a cotton wool. To remove the dry-cleaning fluid, apply a damp soapy sponge repeatedly until no odour remains. Use paper towels to dry as much as you can, then dry the mattress in the sun. If you can't get the mattress in the sun, dry it with a hairdryer. If any odour remains, dampen the area with a cloth, cover with talcum powder and allow the powder to absorb the last of the odour. Vacuum.

Problem: **Semen stain on the mattress.**
What to use: **Bar of soap, cloth, ice.**
How to apply: Dampen a bar of soap with cold water and rub it over the stain. Leave it for 2 minutes then rub the soap off with a damp cloth. Allow to dry. For old semen stains, ice the stain before applying soap.

Q: 'My child is a bed-wetter,' reports Jane. 'Urine has soaked into his mattress. What do you suggest?'

Problem: **Urine stain on mattress.**
What to use: **Detergent, cloth, hairdryer, lemon juice or white vinegar, cloth.**
How to apply: Add a little detergent to water to generate a sudsy mix. Scrub the suds into the stain with a cloth and, if you can, put the mattress in the sun. If you can't, use

paper towels to dry as much as you can. Then dry
with a hairdryer. Neutralise the smell with lemon juice
or white vinegar applied sparingly with a damp cloth.

Problem:	**New red-wine stain on mattress.**
What to use:	**Old toothbrush, vinegar, paper towel.**
How to apply:	Dip an old toothbrush in vinegar and rub it over the stain. Blot the stain with paper towels. Repeat until clean. Dry thoroughly.

Problem:	**Old red-wine stain on mattress.**
What to use:	**Glycerine, cotton wool ball, bicarb, vinegar, soft brush, detergent, soapy sponge, paper towel, hairdryer, vacuum cleaner.**
How to apply:	Loosen the stain with glycerine applied with a cotton wool ball until the edge of the stain begins to lighten. Make a paste with 1 dessertspoon of bicarb and 2 dessertspoons of vinegar and scrub into the stain. Wait until it stops fizzing then rub it off with a soft brush. Leave until the stain begins to disappear. Then wipe it off with a damp soapy sponge. Blot with paper towels and dry with a hairdryer. Then vacuum.

Q: 'We've stored an inner-spring mattress in a caravan for six months,' reports Jenny. 'It really smells. What do you suggest?'

Problem:	**Smelly mattress.**
What to use:	**Household steamer, lavender oil, bicarb, vacuum cleaner.**
How to apply:	Hire a household steamer, put a couple of drops of lavender oil in the water and apply the steam to the

entire mattress. A steamer works a bit like a reverse vacuum cleaner. Then put the mattress in the sunshine. If you can, lie it on top of the clothesline so air can circulate around the mattress. If you can't get it into the sun, dust bicarb over the mattress and leave it until it's completely dry, then vacuum. Turn and repeat on the other side. Push up and down on the mattress while sniffing the air vents on the side of the mattress. If smell is released, you need to steam again!

Caring for waterbeds

I know all about waterbeds because I have one. They're particularly helpful for people with arthritis because you don't get pressure points on your joints. I clean them using the '333' technique. Every 3 months add the proprietary chemical to the water. Every 3 months pull the cover off and wash it as you would a duvet. And every 3 months wipe in and around the bag and underneath the plastic reservoir. Make sure you dry the area thoroughly with a towel before returning the bedding.

The water level is crucial. To work out the right level, lie on the bed with your sleeping partner (if you have one). If you both roll into the middle, you need to add more water. If you both roll towards the sides, you need to remove some water. And when you are replacing the water, use warm rather than cold water.

If you get a hole in the bladder, call a professional. I've found that the cost of repairing or replacing the bladder is fairly reasonable and attempting to do it yourself is tricky. Failing to repair it properly will give you a rude shock in the middle of the night and a disaster the next day when you try to dry everything out. Waterbeds hold a lot of water!

Sheets

There's nothing better than getting into bed with clean, fresh sheets. When selecting sheets, choose natural fibres such as cotton, silk or linen. I hate polyester satin sheets. They may look good but they're cold in winter and like lying on a plastic bag in summer! Wash your sheets once a week in a good detergent. If you can, dry them in the sun because it's a great antibacterial and leaves them smelling fresh. I love sheets to have that starchy feel. You can make your own starch from rice. Strain the water after you cook rice and add it to the rinse water in the washing machine. The sheets will be really white and firm against your skin and the rice powder helps prevent sweat.

With accidental spills, work out what the stain is made of and then work out its solvent, remembering that protein stains need to be removed first with cold water before fat stains are removed with hot water. If you do it the other way around, you'll set the protein stain.

Problem:	**Tea stain on sheets.**
What to use:	**Glycerine, cotton wool balls; or glycerine, cotton wool ball, dry-cleaning fluid.**
How to apply:	For fresh stains, rub glycerine into the stain with a cotton wool ball. Then put the sheets through the washing machine on the cold cycle. For old stains, apply glycerine with a cotton wool ball, then rub in dry-cleaning fluid with a cotton wool ball and leave for 10–15 minutes. Then put the sheets through the washing machine on the cold cycle.

Q: 'Most of the time I can't be bothered removing my make-up before I go to bed,' admits Kristie. 'I then often transfer the make-up to my sheets during the night. What's the best way to get it off?'

Problem: Lipstick/greasy make-up stain on sheets.

What to use: Cotton wool balls, methylated spirits; or dry-cleaning fluid, cotton wool balls.

How to apply: Hold a cotton wool ball on the back of the stain, then dip another in methylated spirits and rub it in a circular motion over the stain, working from the outside to the inside of the stain. Replace the dirty cotton wool as needed until the stain is removed. If the lipstick is dark, use dry-cleaning fluid in the same way. Then wash in the washing machine.

Problem: Fruit juice stains on sheets.

What to use: *Vanish*.

How to apply: Wash the sheets in the washing machine and hang them in sunshine. If you can't dry the sheets in the sun, soak them in *Vanish* before washing then tumble dry. If the sheets are white, use *Vanish Oxi Action Crystal White*. If the sheets are coloured, use *Vanish Oxi Action*.

Problem: Candle wax stain on sheets.

What to use: Ice, blunt knife or scissors, dry-cleaning fluid, cotton wool balls, paper towel, iron.

How to apply: Put ice on the wax and remove as much as possible, either with a blunt knife or scissors. Don't damage the fabric! Then apply dry-cleaning fluid with a cotton wool on either side of the wax, working in a circular motion. For any remaining marks, put several layers of paper towel on the ironing board, put the sheet on top, then place more paper towels over the wax and iron over the paper towels. Replace the paper towel regularly until all the wax is removed.

Q: 'I had a cut on my knee which bled through the bandage and onto my sheets,' reveals Jessica. 'I washed the sheets in hot water, which has set the stain. Can it be fixed?'

Problem:	**Bloodstain on sheets.**
What to use:	**Bar of soap; *Vanish*; or glycerine, cotton wool.**
How to apply:	Dampen the soap in cold water and rub over the stain. Then rub the stain against itself vigorously until it's removed. You may need to do this a few times. Put the sheets through the washing machine on the cold cycle. An alternative is to soak the stain in *Vanish*. If the stain has set, apply glycerine with cotton wool to either side of the stain. Rub in circles from the outside to the inside of the stain until it starts to shift at the edge, then wash in *Vanish* and cold water.

Problem:	**Semen stain on sheets.**
What to use:	**Bar of soap.**
How to apply:	Dampen the soap in cold water and rub over the stain. Then rub the stain against itself until it's removed. Wash the sheets on a cold cycle.

Problem:	**Egg yolk stain on sheets.**
What to use:	**Bar of soap, cold water, warm wash.**
How to apply:	Dampen the soap in cold water and rub over the stain. Then put the sheets through the washing machine on a warm setting to remove the fats.

Problem:	**Chocolate stain on sheets.**
What to use:	**Bar of soap; or dry-cleaning fluid, cotton wool.**

How to apply: Dampen the soap in cold water, then rub over the stain before soaking in cold water. Wash the sheets in the washing machine on a warm or hot cycle. If the fabric is polyester satin, use dry-cleaning fluid applied with a cotton wool ball to the stain with another cotton wool ball held at the back of the stain. Rub in a circular motion, working from the outside to the inside of the stain. Then wash normally.

Problem: Ink/ballpoint pen stain on sheets.
What to use: Milk; or dry-cleaning fluid, cotton wool balls.
How to apply: Rot a carton of milk in the sun (the time this takes will vary). Then heap the solids over the stain with your hand. Leave until the ink starts to soak into the solids. Then wash the rotten milk out in the washing machine on the warm cycle. Alternatively, apply dry-cleaning fluid with a cotton wool ball, working in a circular motion from the outside to the inside of the stain. Remove all the colour before placing the sheets in the washing machine on the warm cycle.

Problem: Vomit stain on sheets.
What to use: *Vanish*.
How to apply: Rinse out the solids first with water, then put the sheets through the washing machine and dry them in the sun. If you can't dry them in the sun, soak them in *Vanish* before putting them through the washing machine. Then put them in the dryer. Always wash vomit as soon as possible because mould can grow on it overnight and will stain.

Soundproof your bedroom

I've lived in some really noisy places. I've lived next to train lines, under flight paths, on main roads—even above a massage parlour! You can reduce noise by restricting the sound vibrations. Place objects, such as wardrobes, against the wall to muffle sound. Use heavy curtains, several lightweight curtains or ruffled curtains to minimise noise. Fluffy items help. If noise is coming from underneath, don't lean your bed against the wall and put high-density foam rubber squares under the four corners of your bed. Layering carpets and rugs also helps to reduce noise levels. If the noise is coming from above, hang mosquito nets or parachutes from the ceiling or put up some wall hangings. Put felt spots behind picture frames and mirrors on walls to prevent vibration. You could also put pelmets over windows.

Pillows

I like my pillows in all shapes, sizes and densities. Pillows can be made of foam, feather, polyester or kapoc. Use a pillow protector as well as a pillowcase and wash them weekly. The reason why you should use a protector is to stop the pillow compacting or needing as much washing. Wash pillows in woolwash the same way that you would wash your duvet as described below. Allow them to dry in an elevated area so the water can drip away. The top of the clothesline is ideal. Turn the pillow regularly while it's drying but never compress it while it's wet. When you think it's dry, leave it for another hour to make sure the centre of it has dried completely.

Duvets

Duvets can be made of goose feathers, wool or synthetics. Wash them twice a year or even more if you sweat a lot. You can tell it's time for a wash when the fibres are packed down and lumpy, or the duvet smells. Some duvets can be put through the washing machine. Just check the manufacturer's instructions first. Others, regardless of the filling, can be washed in a bath or large washing sink. If you don't have one, try to borrow a friend's.

Fill the bath with water warmed to blood temperature and half a cap of woolwash for a double-sized duvet. Lay the duvet in the bath then get in yourself and stomp up and down on the duvet until you get rid of all the dirt and grime. Empty the bath, fill it again with clean, blood-heat water and stomp over it again. Let the water out, fill the bath again with clean, blood-heat water and allow it to soak through the duvet.

After you've rinsed the duvet, drain the water from the bath and tread on the duvet to squeeze out as much moisture as possible. Place the duvet in a large black bin bag rather than a basket so you don't leave a drip trail. Then take the duvet outside and put it on an old sheet. If you don't have a lawn, place it flat over the top of the clothesline. Leave it to dry for quite some time, then shake it and turn it. You need to do this about three times until it's almost dry. Then hang it on the clothesline using lots of pegs so you don't put stress on any one spot. Unless you already have a stitched ridge, don't fold the duvet over the line. Instead, peg it by the two outside edges on separate lines so that it forms a U-shape. This allows air to circulate. When it's almost completely dry, whack it with your hand or an old tennis racquet. This fluffs up the fibres or loosens the feathers. Then put it back inside the duvet cover to protect it against spills and grime.

If you can't be bothered washing your duvet, at least hang it on the clothesline in the sun to allow the UV rays to kill bacteria.

Blankets

Blankets should be aired regularly, preferably once a week, and outside if possible. Woollen blankets should be washed once every 4–6 months in shampoo and conditioner – the cheaper, the better, because they contain less perfume. For single-sized blankets, use 3 dessertspoons of shampoo with water warmed to blood temperature, rinse, then use 3 dessertspoons of conditioner with water warmed to blood temperature. Use double the amount for double-sized blankets. After rinsing, dry them in the morning sun or dappled shade, not the afternoon sun, or the blankets will stiffen.

Machine wash only if the manufacturer's instructions indicate that you can. If you use the washing machine, add 1–1½ caps of woolwash for a double blanket. If you wash the blanket in the bath, use 2 caps of woolwash or shampoo. Don't leave blankets to soak. Just wash them in blood-heat water, rinse in blood-heat water and hang to dry. If you agitate woollen blankets too much, the blanket will shrink, leaving you with a felt wad instead of a soft blanket.

Cotton blankets can be machine washed the same way as sheets. Faux mink blankets can either be hand washed with woolwash or shampoo in blood-heat water or dry cleaned. Make sure you brush with a hairbrush as it dries.

Never put sheepskin in the washing machine or agitate it. Instead, wash sheepskin underblankets with woolwash or shampoo in a bath, sink or bucket. Dry them lying flat. Just before the sheepskin is completely dry, brush it with a hairbrush in all directions.

Read the washing instructions before cleaning an electric blanket. If it doesn't have any instructions, take it to a reputable dry cleaner.

If you have space, store blankets in a blanket box or, better still, a camphor wood box because this will keep insects away. Otherwise, keep blankets in the cupboard but protect them with some camphor inside a handkerchief and plastic bag. Prick little holes in the plastic and put it inside your blankets. This will keep insects and other nasties away but won't mark your blankets. Store duvets the same way.

DRAWERS AND WARDROBES

Drawers and wardrobes take many forms. They can be built-in or stand alone, old or new. Those with a shellac, French polish or varnish finish should be cleaned once a month with a good quality, silicone-free furniture polish. Just put a small amount of polish on a cloth, wipe it over the piece, then wipe it off with the other side of the cloth. A good furniture polish should remove most small scratches.

Those with a laminate or polyurethane finish can be cleaned with a damp cloth. If they're very dirty, use bicarb and vinegar. Keep polyurethane pieces away from windows because the sun's UV rays will yellow them.

To clean the inside of drawers, take your clothes out and vacuum. If the area is very dirty, use vinegar and water on a sponge. To deter nasties, put some lavender oil or tea-tree oil on a cloth and wipe over the drawer or cupboard interior. A cake of soap left in the drawer will also deter bugs and scent your clothes. You can also buy scented and anti-bug drawer liners to fit into your drawers. These will also protect your clothes from the tannins in the wood.

If you apply make-up at a dressing table with a wooden surface, protect it with a glass tile or mirror tile. A mirror tile is preferable because it gives backlighting and your make-up will be applied perfectly. I also like to put foam in my bedside table drawers so that if I drop make-up bottles or jewellery, they won't break!

Problem:	**Sticking drawers in furniture.**
What to use:	**Soap or candle wax; or *Gumption*, sponge.**
How to apply:	Take the drawer out. If it has wooden runners, rub them with soap. You can also use rub candle wax

along the runners. For plastic runners, polish with *Gumption* on a sponge. If this doesn't work, your chest of drawers may be uneven. You can check this with a spirit level horizontally and vertically. If it is not level, put some cardboard or a small block of wood under one of the legs to steady it. You could also have a problem with the backing sheet of the drawer, which may need to be refastened or replaced if it's buckled. A lot of modern furniture is built with cheap backing sheets and if they buckle it takes the drawers out of alignment. It's easy to check this by looking at the back of the cupboard and making sure the sheets are flush to the edge. You can replace them yourself or get professional help. Also check that the joints of the drawer are secure. If you're re-painting your drawers, don't paint the sides of each drawer or they will stick!

Q: 'How do you remove beeswax from a wardrobe?' asks Bill.

Problem:	**Beeswax on wardrobe.**
What to use:	**Mineral turpentine, water, cloth.**
How to apply:	Mix 1 part mineral turpentine with 1 part water and wipe the mixture over the beeswax with a cloth.

Q: 'My cast-iron chest has gone rusty,' reports David. 'Can it be fixed?'

Problem:	**Rust on cast-iron chest.**
What to use:	**Rubber gloves, rust converter, roller, methylated spirits, cloth.**

How to apply: Don't scrub the rust first because there'll be nothing
left to convert! Put on rubber gloves, then apply the
rust converter with a brush, rag, sponge or roller.
Apply sparingly. You'll know if you've used too much
if you get a white powdery coating. If this happens,
wash it off with methylated spirits on a cloth.

How to hang clothes in the wardrobe

Most people have a system for sorting out where their clothes go
in the wardrobe. But if you don't, and you're tired of wasting time
searching for that shirt you know is in there somewhere, this is what
I do.

Clothes last longer if they're hung rather than folded, so hang
as much as you can. The exception is woollens and knits, which
should be stored flat.

Use good coathangers. Wooden hangers are the best,
plastic are OK and wire coathangers need to be wrapped with
foam strips or old shoulder pads pinned on the shoulders of the
hanger.

Divide your wardrobe into sections, putting similar types of
clothes together. All your shirts should be together, for example.
Then order the sections by size, putting the longest garments at
one end and the shortest at the other end. You can further sort
your clothes by colour. One suggestion is by the colours of the
rainbow. Then order by sleeve length and seasonal weight.

The beauty of this system is that if your skirt is not in the
wardrobe, then it's in the wash or at the dry cleaners. You won't
spend hours searching.

Problem: Moths in the wardrobe.
What to use: Camphor ball, cloves, lavender, eucalyptus oil,
small muslin bag.

How to apply: Place 1 camphor ball, 4 cloves, a sprig of lavender and a couple of drops of eucalyptus oil into a small muslin bag. Tie it, then hang it on the rod in your wardrobe. You'll deter silverfish, moths, dust mites and other insects and keep your clothes smelling fresh. Replace eucalyptus and lavender every two months. Replace the others yearly.

Q:

'When you've had your clothes sitting on a coathanger for a while, the hanger can leave a mark,' reports Terzine. 'If you don't have time to iron it out, is there anything you can do?'

Problem: Hanger marks on clothes.
What to use: Spray bottle, body heat.
How to apply: Before you put the garment on, damp spray the spot with water where the hanger has left its indentation. When you put the garment on, your body heat will interact with the water and smooth the marks out. To prevent the problem, wrap the shoulder line of your coathanger with foam strips or old shoulder pads.

CLOTHING

My mother has a horror of anything that itches – and she passed this on to me in spades. Clothes have to be soft on your skin and finished properly. Anything with a lace edge has to have a cotton lawn bias binding or silk bias binding stitched over the seams. It's a practice I've adopted. Of course you're going to get spills and stains on your clothes, they're a barrier between you and the world. Start by working out what's in the stain. If it has several components, remove proteins first, then fats, then chemicals.

Q: 'My cotton business shirts have sweat stains that just won't wash out,' says Steve. 'Do you have a suggestion on what to do because the shirts aren't cheap?'

Problem:	**Sweat marks on fabric.**
What to use:	*Vanish Oxi Action.*
How to apply:	Make a paste with *Vanish Oxi Action* and water to the consistency of peanut butter and apply this to the stain. Leave for 15 mintues before washing. You must use *Vanish Oxi Action* rather than just *Vanish*.

Q: 'My deodorant has left white stains on my shirts,' says Susie. 'It's like it's permanently caked on now. Can I remove this?'

Problem:	**Deodorant stains on fabric.**
What to use:	*Vanish Oxi Action.*
How to apply:	Make a paste with *Vanish Oxi Action* and water to the consistency of peanut butter. Apply it to the deodorant stains and leave for 15 minutes, then wash the shirts as usual in the washing machine.

Q: 'My husband was wearing suntan cream and it's marked the neckline of his shirt,' says Sandra. 'Can I get it off?'

Problem:	**Suntan cream on fabric.**
What to use:	*Vanish Oxi Action.*
How to apply:	Make a paste of *Vanish Oxi Action* and water to the consistency of peanut butter and apply it to the stain. Leave it to penetrate for 15 minutes then wash in the washing machine as usual.

Q: 'I'm a bachelor,' says Geoffrey. 'And I accidentally put my jumper into the washing machine and it's shrunk. Can it be fixed?'

Problem:	Shrunken jumper.
What to use:	Bucket, Fuller's Earth, towel, two wide-toothed combs; or Epsom salts.
How to apply:	For dark-coloured jumpers, fill a nappy-sized bucket with blood-heat water and add 2 tablespoons of Fuller's Earth. For light-coloured jumpers, add 4 tablespoons. Put the jumper in and gently agitate it with your hands until it's thoroughly wetted. Let it sit for 10–15 minutes and then rinse thoroughly in blood-heat water. Don't leave it for longer than this or it will bleach. Lie the jumper flat on a towel in a shady spot and leave it to dry. Gently stretch it back into shape as it's drying. To make it stretch more evenly, use two wide-toothed combs on either side of the jumper and stretch the jumper with the combs as it's drying. It's not as effective, but you could also use 2 tablespoons of Epsom salts, instead of Fuller's Earth, to a bucket of blood-heat water.

Q: 'I hate the dressing on new shirts,' says Stephen. 'Is there a way you can soften them so they're like your old favourite shirts?'

Problem:	How to soften stiff or brand new shirts.
What to use:	Bicarb, washing powder, vinegar.
How to apply:	Put the shirts through the washing machine, adding 60 g of bicarb to your washing powder and 120 ml of vinegar to the rinse water.

Q:

'I pulled out an old cream satin evening gown which was covered in mildew,' says Barbara. 'Is it fixable?'

Problem:	**Mildew on satin.**
What to use:	**Hairdryer, clothes brush, salt.**
How to apply:	Blow a hairdryer over the satin until it is warm. This causes the mildew to blow up and fluff up. Then rub a clothes brush in the direction of the watery-looking part of the satin. If any black marks remain, cover them with dry salt and brush backwards and forwards with a clothes brush. Then brush off.

Problem:	**Stretched cotton-knit jumper.**
What to use:	**Wide-toothed comb, Fuller's Earth.**
How to apply:	Use a wide-toothed comb to evenly stretch the jumper. Then put it in the washing machine on the hot water setting. Before it reaches the spin cycle, remove the jumper and put it in the dryer. The water superheats and shrinks the fibres. You can also add 1 tablespoon of Fuller's Earth to the wash cycle to help shrink it.

How to stop angora jumpers shedding

To stop angora jumpers from shedding, put them in the freezer for 20 minutes before wearing them. Or add a little hair conditioner the size of a 10-pence piece to the rinse water when you're washing them.

Q: 'How do you remove chocolate ice cream from a T-shirt?' asks Maureen.

Problem:	**Chocolate ice-cream on T-shirt.**
What to use:	**Bar of soap.**
How to apply:	As the chocolate contains protein, you must use cold water. Vigorously rub the stain with the soap and cold water. Then wash normally.

Problem:	**Shine on a suit.**
What to use:	**Cloth, white vinegar, bran, brown paper, iron.**
How to apply:	For a dark-coloured suit, dampen a cloth in vinegar and wipe it over the suit. Then place brown paper over the suit and iron. For light-coloured suits, dampen a cloth in 1 part white vinegar to 4 parts water, wring it out and lay it over the shiny section of the suit. Steam-iron the suit.

Q: 'We were at Carols by Candlelight and wax dripped onto my husband's corduroy trousers,' says Kay. 'We tried putting ice onto it and it didn't work!'

Problem:	**Wax on corduroy fabric.**
What to use:	**Paper towel, dry-cleaning fluid, cotton wool balls.**
How to apply:	On an ironing board, place a few layers of paper towel on top of one another and then place the trousers on top of them rib side down. Then put more layers of paper towel on top of the stained trousers and run a hot iron over them. The wax will be absorbed by the paper towel. For the final bit of wax, put dry-cleaning fluid onto a cotton wool ball and wipe over the area.

Q: 'My daughter works as a beauty therapist,' says Sandra, 'and she waxes a lot of legs. As a consequence, her black synthetic slacks have wax on them. How should I get it off?'

Problem:	**Wax on synthetic fabric.**
What to use:	**Paper towel, hairdryer.**
How to apply:	Put a paper towel on either side of the wax and blow a hairdryer over the area. The paper towel will absorb the wax. Keep on replacing the paper towel until the wax is removed.

Q: 'My six-year-old daughter wore her brand new white ladybird T-shirt under a walnut tree,' says Megan, 'and bird dropping landed on her. What can I do?'

Problem:	**Bird dropping on fabric.**
What to use:	**Vinegar, glycerine, salt, *Vanish*.**
How to apply:	Walnuts contain a dye that has to be treated with vinegar first, then glycerine. Soak the fabric until the stain begins to move. Rub with glycerine, then salt. Rinse, then wash in *Vanish*.

Problem:	**Tree sap on fabric.**
What to use:	**Cotton wool balls, dry-cleaning fluid.**
How to apply:	Put a dry cotton wool ball behind the stain and dip another ball in dry-cleaning fluid. Wipe it over the stain in a circular motion, going from the outside to the inside of the stain. Then wash normally.

Q: 'I'm a banana cutter,' reveals Kevin, 'and I've got banana sap all over my clothes. Can I get it out?'

Problem:	**Banana sap on fabric.**
What to use:	**Glycerine, cotton wool balls, dry-cleaning fluid.**
How to apply:	Apply glycerine to the stain with cotton wool to remove the latex in the sap, then apply dry-cleaning fluid with another ball to remove oxides. Then wash normally.

If you get grease on fabric, there are two methods of cleaning them, described below. If the problem is recurring, use the first method.

Q: 'I work in the transport industry,' says Tom, 'and I'm always getting grease on my clothes. What should I do?'

Problem:	**Grease on fabric.**
What to use:	**Baby oil, cotton wool ball, *Vanish*.**
How to apply:	Baby oil is a mineral oil that breaks down grease. Put baby oil on a cotton wool ball and apply it to the grease. Rub it in circles. Then soak the garment in *Vanish* and hot water before washing.

Q: 'My daughter was given a new nightie by her nanna,' says Patrick, 'but I'd been washing grease off my truck and it ended up on the nightie. Needless to say, I'm not too popular. Can the nightie be fixed?'

Problem:	**Grease on fabric.**
What to use:	**Dry-cleaning fluid, cotton wool balls, oxygen-based bleach.**

How to apply: This is a difficult job. Rub the spots first with dry-cleaning fluid applied with a cotton wool ball. Then soak the nightie in oxygen-based bleach. It may be easier to buy a new pair of pyjamas.

Q: 'My car broke down the other day and, as I was looking under it, I got tar and gravel over my shorts,' says Frank. 'Can I get it off?'

Problem: Tar on fabric.

What to use: Scissors or blade, baby oil, cotton wool balls, kerosene or dry-cleaning fluid.

How to apply: If you can, place the fabric in the freezer. Then cut off as much tar as possible with scissors or a blade. Then dampen the back of the stain with baby oil on a cotton wool ball. Let it soak for a little while and then rub the front of the stain with a cotton wool ball dipped in either kerosene or dry-cleaning fluid. Make sure you work from the outside to the inside of the stain. Use clean cotton wool balls, one after the other, until the tar is removed. Do not heat tar or it will spread.

Problem: Hair dye on fabric.

What to use: Cotton wool ball, cotton bud, dry-cleaning fluid or kerosene, hairspray.

How to apply: Place a cotton wool ball behind the hair dye, dip a cotton bud in dry-cleaning fluid or kerosene and rub the stain off. Spraying hairspray will work as well, but only if you use it immediately, as hairdressers do.

Q: 'I used to get rust off my sailing clothes with a product called *Rustyban*,' reports David. 'It was taken off the market and I'm wondering what I can use now.'

Problem:	**Rust on fabric.**
What to use:	**Cotton wool ball, cotton bud, descaler; or lemon juice and salt.**
How to apply:	*Rustyban* was withdrawn from the market because it was toxic. Try descaler instead. Put a cotton wool ball behind the stain and dip a cotton bud in descaler. Rub it over the rust until it starts to lift. Then hand wash the garment straight away – the rust should come off. Descaler is a very strong product so be careful. If you'd rather use something natural, try lemon juice and salt. Dampen the rust spot with lemon juice and then rub salt over it until the rust starts to move from the fibres. Hand wash and begin the process again until all the rust comes out. This could take some time.

Q: 'During a blackout, I managed to back into a freshly painted wall,' reports Rodney. 'Now I've got paint marks on the seat of my trousers. Can I fix it?'

Problem:	**Paint on fabric.**
What to use:	**Turpentine, methylated spirits, acetone, cotton bud, cotton wool balls.**
How to apply:	To work out what kind of paint it is, get three small containers – one each for turpentine, methylated spirits and acetone. Dip a separate cotton bud in each and apply it to the stains, then rub the stain

between your thumb and your forefinger. Whichever takes colour is the solvent.

The paint is most likely water-based. Because it has dried, soak the stained area with methylated spirits. Then soak two cotton wool balls in methylated spirits and place them on either side of the fabric. Rub the top cotton wool ball in a circular motion, working from the outside to the inside of the stain. Then wash the trousers as you would normally. If the paint is oil-based, use mineral turpentine or acetone in the same way.

Q: 'When I was travelling, the blue from my asthma pack rubbed onto my yellow polyester viscose trousers,' says Jocelynne. 'Can I get it off?'

Problem:	**Ink stain on fabric.**
What to use:	**Milk; or dry-cleaning fluid, cotton wool ball.**
How to apply:	Rot a carton of milk in the sun and spread the solids over the stain. Leave until the ink begins to rise into the milk solids. Then wash the rotten milk out in the washing machine. Alternatively, apply dry-cleaning fluid with a cotton wool ball, working in a circular motion from the outside to the inside of the stain until it's removed. Then wash normally.

Q: 'I buy a lot of second-hand clothes,' says Joyce. 'But they often have a musty smell about them. What do you suggest?'

Problem:	**Musty smell on clothes.**
What to use:	**Tea bag.**

How to apply: The musty smell is caused by dust mites and mildew. To get rid of it, put a tea bag into the washing machine after the water has filled, but before it starts agitating. Hold the bag in the water for 2 minutes then remove. The tannins in the tea kill dust mites. If you suffer dust mite allergy, keep a damp tea bag in a plastic bag in your handbag to sniff when you're in second-hand stores. It'll stop you from sneezing.

Problem: **Dirty woollen coats, dresses or skirts.**
What to use: **Salt, clean handkerchief or piece of linen, bristle brush.**
How to apply: This is an alternative to dry cleaning and much cheaper. Sprinkle the item with salt about as thickly as poppy seeds on bread. Then rub with a clean handkerchief or piece of linen. Don't go in circles but up and down with the grain of the fabric. Once the item is clean, give it a really good shake and brush with a bristle brush.

 'My mum gave me her old mink jacket,' says Jo. 'I have no idea how to clean it.'

Problem: **Cleaning fur or faux fur coats.**
What to use: **Pillowcase, wheat bran.**
How to apply: Place the coat in a large pillowcase and add 1 kg of bran. Secure the top of the pillowcase and shake vigorously for about 3 minutes. Open the pillowcase and lightly shake the item as you remove it, so the bran stays in the pillowcase. This technique is also good for wool, mohair or camel coats and is a quick way to clean suits.

Silk

The best way to wash silk is with shampoo and with conditioner in
the rinse water. Use the same amount as you would with your hair.
Never dry silk on a windy day because all the fibres go stiff and
cause white dusty marks, white lines and water marks.

Problem:	**Water marks on silk.**
What to use:	**Clean white silk square.**
How to apply:	As taught to me by my grandmother, rub the clean white silk square gently across and down the grain of the silk. Don't rub diagonally.

Problem:	**White lines on silk.**
What to use:	**Vinegar, salt.**
How to apply:	When hand washing silk, put vinegar into the rinse water and the white lines won't appear. To keep silk soft, put a teaspoon of salt in the washing water.

Q: 'I'm not sure if it's coffee or red wine,' admits Les,
'but it's stained the elbow of my white raw-silk
jacket. I took it to the dry cleaners and the stain is
still there. Can it be fixed?'

Problem:	**Coffee or red wine stain on silk.**
What to use:	**Glycerine, cotton wool balls, dry-cleaning fluid.**
How to apply:	If it's an old red wine or old coffee stain use glycerine first. Apply it with cotton wool balls on both sides of the fabric and leave for a few minutes. Then use dry-cleaning fluid applied with cotton wool balls, working in a circular motion from the outside to the inside of the stain. If you spill red wine or coffee on

clothing, treat it straight away with white vinegar then take it to the dry cleaner.

Q:
'I splashed black coffee over my favourite silk tie,' says Geoff. *'It just won't shift!'*

Problem:	**Coffee stain on silk.**
What to use:	**Glycerine, cotton wool ball, washing power, vinegar, towel.**
How to apply:	Apply glycerine to the stain with a cotton wool ball. Then wash the tie with washing powder in blood-heat water. Rinse in blood-heat water and, to prevent the tie stiffening, add a little vinegar. Then dry it flat on a towel in the shade.

Leather

Problem:	**Oily stains on suede.**
What to use:	**Dry-cleaning fluid, cotton bud or cotton wool ball, talcum powder, soft bristle brush; or bran, vinegar.**
How to apply:	Dampen the stain with dry-cleaning fluid applied with a cotton bud or cotton wool ball, then cover the dry-cleaning fluid with talcum powder and allow to dry. Brush the talcum powder out with a soft bristle brush. Repeat if necessary. You can clean suede by rubbing bran over it. Remove sweat marks by dampening some vinegar on the marks, then rub with bran.

How to repair a small hole in a leather jacket

Most people have a leather jacket for life unless it was one of those bat-wing 1980s numbers. Getting a hole is usually devastating, but here's how you can keep the jacket alive.

Find a matching piece of leather. This could be taken from the inside of the hemline or seam or under an armpit seam. Cut a paper template 1 millimetre larger than the shape of the hole, place it on top of the leather piece and cut around it to make the patch. Sand the back of the leather patch with sandpaper so that you thin the edges. On a piece of linen or cotton that is 1 cm larger all round than the leather patch apply malleable contact adhesive or specialist leather adhesive and glue on the patch.

The patch will now be sitting in the middle of the sticky, adhesive-covered piece of linen or cotton. Line the patch up with the back of the hole and attach. You'll find it's a little thick where the two layers overlap. Lay the face of the leather on a smooth surface such as a breadboard and tap the back of it with a flat-headed hammer. The leather will smooth out and appear to be one piece of leather again.

Turn it over again so you're looking at the front. Warm a spoon, dip the back of it in a little *Vaseline* and lightly rub the patched area. For hard leather surfaces, use paraffin wax.

Q: Angela loves her old red leather jacket, 'I've had it for years. But it's got deodorant smeared on it. Is there any way I can get this off?'

Problem:	**Deodorant on leather.**
What to use:	**Dry-cleaning fluid, cotton bud, talcum powder, leather dew.**
How to apply:	Apply dry-cleaning fluid to the smears with a cotton bud, then sprinkle with talcum powder. Allow it to absorb, then clean the jacket with leather dew (following the directions on the packet).

Q: 'How do you get chewing gum off a leather jacket?' asks Victor.

Problem:	Chewing gum on leather.
What to use:	Ice, scissors or a blade, dry-cleaning fluid, cotton bud, sticky tape, leather dew.
How to apply:	Put ice on the gum. Once it has hardened, cut as much off as possible with scissors or a blade, but be careful not to cut the surface of the leather. Then apply dry-cleaning fluid with a cotton bud. Remove the last of the gum with sticky tape. Keep on ripping the sticky tape away as though you're waxing a leg. Do this until all the gum has been removed. Then treat the spot with leather dew.

Zips

Problem:	Sticky zips.
What to use:	Vinegar, lead pencil, graphite powder or glycerine, talcum powder.
How to apply:	For metal zips, apply some vinegar to the zip then rub the metal with a lead pencil or apply graphite powder. Work it up and down. Graphite isn't as effective as a lead pencil, because it doesn't contain clay, but it will work with a little persistence. For nylon zips, apply some glycerine, working it up and down. Then sprinkle with talcum powder.

Problem:	Loose zips.
What to use:	Salt.
How to apply:	To make zips stick, add a little salt to them. This works with both metal or nylon zips.

Q:

'The zip on my sailing jacket has salt build-up on it,' says William. 'Can it be fixed?'

Problem:	Salt on metal zip.
What to use:	Cloth, vinegar, lead pencil.
How to apply:	Wipe the zip with a cloth dipped in vinegar first, then rub it with a lead pencil.

BAGS

The great thing about a bag is you don't have go on a diet to wear one. They really are 'one size fits all'! I love handbags that can store as much as possible, the bigger the better and the more the merrier. Store bags in a cool dry place covered in a calico bag or old pillowcase.

Problem:	Smelly leather handbag/suitcase.
What to use:	Tea leaves, leather dew.
How to apply:	The bag may smell because it wasn't tanned properly or is made of goat or kangaroo hide. To get rid of the smell, wipe the leather with damp tea leaves. This will cure the leather. Then treat it with leather dew. If the interior of the bag is made of leather and also smells, empty a packet of dry tea leaves into it and leave for a couple of weeks.

Problem:	Mouldy handbag.
What to use:	Vinegar, cloths, oil of cloves, leather dew; or dry-cleaning fluid, cotton wool, talcum powder, brush.
How to apply:	Mix a small quantity of vinegar and water and wipe it over the mould with a cloth. Then wipe with a clean cloth. Add 1 drop of oil of cloves to leather dew on a cloth and wipe over the bag. The oil of cloves will inhibit further mould growth. For black or

old mould stains, apply dry-cleaning fluid with a
cotton wool ball and sprinkle talcum powder over
the top. Once it's dried, brush the talcum powder off.

Problem:	**Dirty handbag lining.**
What to use:	**Washing powder; or dry-cleaning fluid, cotton wool ball.**
How to apply:	Some bag linings can be removed. Others are attached but can still be pulled outside the bag. If the lining is cotton, clean it with washing powder and water. If there's lipstick, make-up or ballpoint pen marks apply dry-cleaning fluid with a cotton wool ball. Then clean in washing powder and water. To dry, put the leather part of the bag in the shade and the lining in the sun. If you can't do this, dry the whole bag in the shade. The lining must be completely dry before you put it back inside the bag.

SHOES

If you're feeling lazy about looking after your shoes, just think about
how much it will cost to replace them.

Store very good shoes in a shoe bag or calico bag to stop them
from going mouldy. After wearing leather and vinyl shoes, dust the
insides of them with a little bicarb. Wipe the outside with a cloth that's
been smeared with *Vaseline*. Bicarb reduces the amount of sweat your
feet produces and the *Vaseline* makes shoes waterproof. Just don't
forget to dust out the bicarb before you wear the shoes again.

Dust bicarb into cloth and running shoes and vacuum it out before
wearing them. Most cloth shoes can be hand or machine washed.
Sprinkle talcum powder on rubber soles and the outside of rubber
boots to stop them perishing.

Clean suede shoes with a brass wire brush (not aluminium or steel wire) and dry-cleaning fluid. Spray suede and cloth shoes with Scotchguard to keep them clean for longer and waterproof. For nubuck or super suede shoes, purchase a small proprietary brand sandblock for cleaning.

Keep the ankles of boots unwrinkled and firm by putting an old paper towel roll inside them so they don't flop over.

Make sure you use the correct shoelaces on shoes. If they're too thin, you place strain on the holes. If they're too thick, you place strain on the front of the shoe. The lace should move through the hole with a light resistance, not a drag nor a run.

If you get a hole in the sole of your shoe, put newspaper on the inside of the sole and use a product called Spread-a-sole. Apply it in several thin coats and it will form a new sole.

If nail heads are coming through your shoes it means your heels may need to be replaced or boosted. Hammer the nails back in, making sure you cover the head of the nail with a small piece of wood.

Serious scuff marks can be removed with leather dew or boot polish rubbed on with the back of a hot spoon. For suede shoes, use dry-cleaning fluid applied with a cotton bud. Sprinkle with talcum powder and brush off.

Q: 'I was in a busy pub and someone's drink landed on my expensive new leather shoes. What can I do?'

Problem:	Beer on leather shoes
What to use:	Glycerine, cotton wool ball, dry-cleaning fluid, cotton bud, talcum powder, brush.
How to apply:	Apply glycerine to the stain with a cotton wool ball. Then apply dry-cleaning fluid with a cotton bud.

Sprinkle over with talcum powder to absorb the dry-cleaning fluid. When completely dry, brush off.

Problem:	**Rubber soles are perishing.**
What to use:	**Salt, stiff brush; or cloudy ammonia, water, salt, stiff brush.**
How to apply:	Scour the rubber with salt and a stiff brush. This will rejuvenate them. Alternatively, use a combination of 1 part cloudy ammonia, 5 parts water and 1 part salt and scrub with a stiff brush.

Q: 'My wife was filling up the car with petrol and she got splashback all over her leather shoes,' reports Brian. 'She loves those shoes.'

Problem:	**Petrol on leather shoes.**
What to use:	**Dry-cleaning fluid, cotton wool ball, talcum powder.**
How to apply:	Apply dry-cleaning fluid with a cotton wool ball to the affected area. Then sprinkle talcum powder over dry-cleaning fluid to absorb it. Leave the shoes until they're dry then brush off the talcum powder.

Problem:	**Velcro not working.**
What to use:	**Fine-toothed comb.**
How to apply:	Dampen the velcro with water and comb it on both sides with a fine-toothed comb. This gets the fluff and dust out.

Q: 'I was at the supermarket and a woman dropped a jar of cucumbers on the ground and the oil splattered onto my shoes,' reports David. 'Can I fix them?'

Problem:	**Oil on shoes.**
What to use:	**Dry-cleaning fluid, cotton wool, talcum powder.**
How to apply:	Put dry-cleaning fluid onto a cotton wool ball and wipe it over the stain on the shoes. Then cover this area with talcum powder, which will absorb the oil. When it's dry, brush the powder off.

How to care for stockings

You wouldn't bother doing this with cheap stockings, but it's worth it with expensive ones. Put soap in one toe and your hand in the other toe and then rub them together as though you're washing your hands. This stretches the fibres and removes more dirt. To prevent ladders and catches in stockings, spray them with hairspray and leave them on a hanger to dry. You'll need to reapply the hairspray each time you wash them.

HATS

I collect hats in many different styles, from Georgian to contemporary. I even have a pop-up silk top hat! Special hats should be stored in a hatbox or on a hat block and kept on a flat surface. If the hat has a high crown and you don't have a hat block, pack it with acid-free tissue paper. Great-aunt Letitia loved wearing berets and taught me how to clean them through her amazing notes. Hand wash woollen berets in woolwash and dry them over a dinner plate so they retain their shape. To bleach a straw hat, rub it with dry-cleaning fluid and a little salt then rub the mixture off well.

Problem: **Sweat marks on felt hats.**
What to use: **Fuller's Earth or plaster of paris, paintbrush, brush.**
How to apply: Sweat on light-coloured hats can be removed with Fuller's Earth. Mix Fuller's Earth and water to the consistency of soft butter. Then paint it over the sweat marks with a paintbrush, leave to dry and then brush out. For dark-coloured felt hats use plaster of paris made to the consistency of soft butter. Put the mixture over the sweat stain with a paint-brush and allow it to dry completely before brushing it off.

Problem: **Straw hat has gone floppy.**
What to use: **Pastry brush, egg white, towels, cling film.**
How to apply: Dip a pastry brush in egg white and wipe both sides of the hat with it. Put towels in the crown of the hat, cover a flat surface with cling film, sit the hat on top and allow it to dry hard.

Q: 'I'm a fan of felt hats,' says Simon, 'but mine seems to have shrunk. Can it be stretched?'

Problem: **Felt hat has shrunk.**
What to use: **Fuller's Earth, hat block or damp newspaper.**
How to apply: Mix Fuller's Earth and water to the consistency of peanut butter. Spread it over the areas that need to be stretched and leave for about 5 minutes. Then force the hat over a suitably sized hat block or pack the inside of the crown with damp newspaper until it's the right size. Leave to dry in the shade, not the sun. The drying time will depend on the thickness of the hat.

JEWELLERY

Use nothing more than a little water to clean absorbent precious stones such as jade, opal, some agates, cloudy quartz and emerald.

Pearls should only be cleaned in a mild salt solution – 1 teaspoon of salt for 600 millilitres of water.

Ivory can be cleaned with sweet almond oil on a cotton bud. Other jewellery should be cleaned with a proprietary product.

Always wipe earring hooks with methylated spirits and a cotton wool ball to remove bacteria.

Never use heat or chemicals on jewellery. If in doubt, take it to a jeweller.

Jewellery boxes

Clean jewellery boxes as you would other furniture. The easiest way to clean the inside is to vacuum it. Just make sure you cover the vacuum cleaner tube with an old T-shirt just in case you suck up a stone! I came up with this solution after dropping a small box with about 30 small gemstones in it that had all been collected from old pieces of jewellery. I dropped the box on a multicoloured, long-pile carpet. The stones are now a gorgeous necklace!

Kids' Stuff

Children are a great source of joy, but also a great source of mess. Whether it's cleaning up after a projectile vomit, removing a drawing from the wall or getting rid of food that's as hard as cement, we've got the solutions for you.

JUST A LITTLE ACCIDENT: MATTHEW'S STORY

Incident: 'My toddler has just moved on from nappies. He's going pretty well but sometimes he gets really excited, forgets there's no nappy and pees. The problem is that the urine runs into his shoes and smells awful. Is there anything I can do?'

Solution: Dab the stain with some dry-cleaning fluid applied with a cotton wool ball. Then sprinkle talcum powder over the dry-cleaning fluid both inside and outside the shoe. Allow to dry and then brush. To neutralise the smell, put lemon juice on a cloth and wipe it over the shoes. Cloth and vinyl shoes can be washed in the washing machine or hand washed and dried in the sunshine.

COTS

Every parent, including me, has a story about messy cots. Ideally, mattresses should be aired every day. This just involves removing the sheets, which you can hang over the side of the cot. It's a good idea to stand the mattress on its end once a week and, if you can, place it in the sun. Sunshine is a fantastic killer of bacteria. Turn the mattress over when you return it to the cot. If you have any spills or stains, sponge them as quickly as possible and stand the mattress up to dry. Use a child-safe mattress protector that has a zip rather than elastic to hold it.

Q: 'My baby vomited in her cot. It went all over the sheets and all through the mattress,' reports Kate. 'She only drinks milk and eats vegetables but it's incredible how much mess a small baby can produce. I've already scrubbed the surface of the mattress and it still smells. What can I do?'

Problem:	**Vomit on sheets.**
What to use:	**Lemon juice, water, spray pack.**
How to apply:	If you can, put the mattress in the sun—this will dry it out and kill bacteria. Wash the sheets in the washing machine and dry them in the sun. To get rid of the smell, mix 1 tablespoon of lemon juice with 1 litre of water in a spray pack and spray it over the mattress. Leave in the sun to dry.

HARD FURNISHINGS

Clean hard furnishings and hard toys with 1 teaspoon of tea-tree oil added to 1 litre of water in a spray bottle. Wipe it off with a cloth. Tea-tree is a great disinfectant and is non-toxic.

HIGHCHAIRS

Wipe highchairs straight after using them and before the food sets. Mix a couple of drops of tea-tree oil with warm water and sponge clean. If you haven't been able to clean before the *Weetabix*, rusks or arrowroot biscuits have become as hard as cement, place a sponge in hot water, wring it and then let it sit over the hardened food for 10 minutes. This will soften the food. Then clean it with tea-tree oil and water.

PRAMS/BUGGIES

Most prams can be cleaned with water. Aluminium buggies need special care because they can become smell traps. Hose or scrub them with 1 teaspoon of detergent or tea-tree oil to 1 litre of water. Do this once a fortnight and then dry the pram in the sun. To clean canvas, mix 225 g of salt in a bucket of water. Apply the solution and scrub with a nylon brush. Leave the buggy in the sun until it's dry, then brush the salt off. In case the buggy runs over some dog poo, run the wheels over a mat or use a damp cloth to wipe them before you go inside.

OLD WICKER FURNITURE

Wicker furniture should be cleaned with a mixture of 1 teaspoon of tea-tree oil to 1 litre of water. Apply with a soft brush. If the furniture is heavily painted, add ½ teaspoon of glycerine to the mix.

CLEANING THE BEDROOM

Children often drop small items like doll accessories or building blocks on their bedroom floor. An easy way to find them is to place either a T-shirt or flywire between the head and tube of the vacuum cleaner. When you vacuum, the item will become trapped and won't go into the bag. Flywire is preferable because you can hear when the item hits it.

If you need to remove felt pen marks from the carpet, use dry-cleaning fluid applied with cotton wool or a cotton bud, depending on how big the stain is. Make sure you rub from the outside to the inside of the stain. Have a dry cloth or chamois block to soak up the dry-cleaning fluid as you go to stop the carpet getting too wet.

Protect carpet in children's rooms by laying down plastic carpet protectors on the floor. You can buy them by the metre at department stores. There are some specially designed for children, with colourful designs and without those nasty spikes.

Another common problem with children is the accidental, or deliberate, placement of stickers on furniture or the wall. These can be removed with a small quantity of detergent and hot water in a spray bottle. Spray the solution over the sticker then place a cling film square over the top and leave for a few minutes. The sticker will come off with the cling film and can be re-stuck where it was supposed to go.

Crayon is very difficult to remove from walls. Use a pencil eraser dampened in a bowl of soapy water and rub it over the crayon. The wax in the crayon will roll off in balls. If the mark is really bad put some bicarb on a damp cotton bud and wipe the mark. Try not to rub outside the crayon mark because it could make the walls go shiny. If it's a large area, use an old toothbrush.

BABY BOTTLES

Wash baby bottles with cold water first to get rid of any remaining milk. Give them a good scrub with a bottlebrush then put them in sterilising solution. The steriliser can give teats a cloudy look. Always rinse sterilising solution with boiled water, particularly with bottles and eating utensils. No baby likes the taste of swimming pool water! The easiest way to fix the awful taste is to rub salt over the cloudy bits and then rinse in boiled water. They're still sterile and the teats stay in better condition.

CLOTH NAPPIES

If you use cloth nappies, clean them with two separate buckets. Fill Bucket 1 with a nappy soak. Fill Bucket 2 with hot water and 1 teaspoon of tea-tree oil. Shake the solids from the nappy into the toilet,

rinse, then put it in Bucket 1. Leave it for 12 hours then swap the nappy
to Bucket 2. Leave it for 20 minutes then put it in the washing machine.
Use hot water in the washing machine and, depending on the size of
the load, add 1 teaspoon to 120 ml of vinegar to the rinse water. Dry in
the sun if possible. If you have to use the dryer, iron the nappies afterwards to kill any bacteria. Bucket 2 and the vinegar clears the soap
residue that often causes nappy rash. If your baby has a rash, rub it
with pawpaw cream. It's a good idea to use nappy liners as well. Nappy
rash in newborns is often caused by plastic pants. Invest in   old-
fashioned woollen flannel pants or fluffies for the first 3 months.

To soften baby clothes, put vinegar in the rinse cycle of the
washing machine to remove the soap residue.

STORING CLOTHES

Put labels on children's drawers to help them learn how to put clothes
away. Include a picture and the name of the clothes to help them.

Q: 'I've been storing baby clothes in the cupboard for
the past four years,' says Petra. 'I need to use them
again but they've gone yellow. Can I get the yellow
out?'

Problem:	**Yellow marks on clothes.**
What to use:	*Vanish*, **bucket, water, acid-free paper.**
How to apply:	The yellow marks are age stains. Add ¾ of a capful of *Vanish* to a 7-litre bucket of warm water and soak overnight. And next time you're packing the clothes away, put a piece of acid-free paper in between each layer of clothing. Age stains come from acid fumes in plastic bags, cardboard boxes or shelving.

STORING TOYS

I'm a big fan of the 'clutter bucket'. Each child (or adult) has their own bucket in a different colour. All their things that become scattered around the house can be collected with the bucket. I also suggest creating your own toy storage out of old cardboard boxes. Spray the boxes with insecticide first, because insects are attracted to cardboard, then paint them. Label them with the name and a picture of what goes into the box so your kids learn to associate the words with the item. It also makes putting toys away a fun activity.

Hang stuffed toys along a line. Get a piece of clothesline twine or cotton sash twine and put plastic pegs along it. Hang the line from shelving units and peg the toys on one after another. Kids love doing this themselves.

Plastic sewing boxes or fishing boxes are great for storing little things like dolly's accessories or nuts and bolts from building sets.

CLEANING TOYS

Wash wooden toys in mild detergent and water but never soak them or the wood will swell. Remove pen marks from wood with dry-cleaning fluid and from plastic with glycerine, both applied with cotton wool.

Read the label to find out how to clean stuffed toys. If you're unsure, vacuum regularly and sponge the surface with tea-tree oil and water to get rid of dust mites.

Plastic toys can be cleaned and sterilised with a mixture of tea-tree oil, glycerine and water.

Fix dolly's hair by combing glycerine through it.

Repair torn pages from books with micropore, which is a fine cotton tape used in bandaging. Micropore is thin enough to read through and doesn't leave yellow lines like sticky tape.

Use a professional cleaner for special or antique toys.

The Laundry

For modern convenience, today's laundry is up there with TV remote controls and Google. It's retreated into a cupboard, the washing line retracts into a wall and both the washing machine and dryer can be operated without interrupting a mobile phone conversation with your sister in Helsinki. But how do you work out which washing powder is the best? And what's the best way to hang your washing? This chapter will reveal all.

REPAIRING A MANKY MINK: KAREN'S STORY

Incident: 'My eleven-year-old son got a synthetic mink blanket
for his birthday last year and he loves it. But I put it
through the washing machine and it's gone all dull
and scratchy. I couldn't bear to tell him and was
going to buy a new one and substitute it. But before I
could, he found the blanket and is really upset. He
even pointed out to me that the washing instructions
indicate hand wash only. Is there a solution?'

Solution: Put ¼ of a bottle (150 ml) of cheap hair conditioner
into a bath filled with blood-heat water. Put the
blanket in and leave it for 1 hour. Don't rinse the
blanket, just hang it in the shade or cover it with a
sheet if it's in the sun. When it's almost dry, brush it
backwards and forwards on both sides with a nylon
or bristle hairbrush. Then leave it to dry completely.

WASHING

I think the washing machine is one of the best inventions. I love
throwing dirty things in and, like magic, getting clean things out.
Here are my general principles for washing clothes:

❏ Use the least amount of chemical and heat to clean. This
helps clothes to last longer.

❏ Wash whites and colours separately. You're less likely to get
that grey look if you further separate colours into pale blues
and greens, put darker blues and greys together, and wash
blacks, browns and reds together. I make a pile of clothes in
each of these colour ranges and wait until there's a full load.

❏ Always make sure the lint filters in the dryer and washing machine are clean. You'll get a better result and it's safer.

❏ Don't overpack the washing machine or dryer. Pack clothes loosely so that that the machine has a chance to agitiate them. Never fill more than $1/3$ of the dryer space with damp clothes.

❏ The best fabric softener is 60 g of bicarb added to the washing powder, then add 120 ml of vinegar to the rinse cycle.

❏ Buy products according to quality rather than cost. A suggested range includes:
  • Good quality washing powder or liquid
  • Oxygen bleach that doesn't bleach colour
  • High whites bleach soaker
  • Antibacterial
  • Woolwash with eucalyptus or cheap shampoo
  • Box pure soap flakes
  • Bottle of cheap hair conditioner

❏ Choose soap powder based on its oxygenated properties and enzyme content. When soap powder comes into contact with water, it creates a chemical reaction and effervesces, allowing bubbles of oxygen to attack stains. Enzymes attack proteins and fats. Cheaper powders tend to have bleaching agents and are not as good for your clothes.

❏ Liquid soap is usually better than powder because fewer particles are left on your clothes. This does vary according to the washing machine with some front loaders performing better with powder.

❏ If you suffer from skin allergies, test the washing powder on your skin before using it on your clothes.

- ❏ If someone in the house has a cold, add 60 ml of lemon juice or 60 ml of vinegar to the rinse water to remove bacteria.
- ❏ Add 60 ml of vinegar to the rinse water if your baby has sensitive skin.

HOT VERSUS COLD WATER

Only use hot water if you have really soiled clothes, otherwise it's not necessary. If the item has normal soiling, use the warm setting. I tend to use the warm setting with a cold rinse. Never use hot water on delicates. Nylons should only be washed in cold water.

Spot cleaning

Dampen the stain with water first. Mix *Vanish Oxi Action* and water to form a paste to the consistency of peanut butter. Leave the paste on the stain for 5–15 minutes and, unless it's hand wash only, put the item through the washing machine.

Starches

The best starch is rice water. Next time you're cooking rice, keep the water after it's boiled. There are two ways of using it. You can either dilute it 1 to 1 with water and put it in a spray bottle ready to apply when you're ironing or you can add it to the rinse water in the washing machine.

Colour run

Dylon's *Runaway* is a good product to use if colour has run in your clothing. If you're dyeing clothes, put 1 teaspoon of bicarb into the dye lot and it will spread more evenly through the fabric.

REMOVING STAINS ON FABRIC

To find out how to remove stains from clothing see pages 155 to 166
in The Bedroom. Below is a kind of ready reference or quick guide to
stain removal from fabrics:

Beer (including dark beer) Paint a paste of *Napisan Oxygen* on the stain and leave for 15 minutes. Then wash normally.

Beetroot Treat with glycerine before washing normally.

Bird droppings Wash fabric normally.

Blood Wash fresh bloodstains through the washing machine on the cold setting. If you can't, use cornflour and water. For old bloodstains, use cold water and soap.

Chewing gum Harden the gum with ice and cut as much off as possible with scissors or a blade. Then apply dry-cleaning fluid with a cotton wool ball, sprinkle talcum powder to absorb it and work the remaining gum out by rubbing in circles.

Chocolate First clean with soap and cold water. Then clean with soap and hot water.

Coffee or tea For fresh stains, use glycerine applied with a cotton wool ball, then wash in washing powder. For old stains, use glycerine, then dry-cleaning fluid and detergent.

Deodorant   Use dry-cleaning fluid before washing.

Egg yolk   Use soap and cold water first, then washing powder and warm water.

Fruit juice   Use detergent and sunshine. For stone fruits and fruits with a high tannin, treat the stain with glycerine first.

Grass   Use dry-cleaning fluid before washing in washing powder.

Grease and oil   Detergent suds. For heavy staining, soak in baby oil first.

Hair dye   Dry-cleaning fluid or kerosene, or hairspray if you can get to the stain immediately.

Ink or ballpoint pen   Rotten milk or dry-cleaning fluid. Use glycerine first on red ink.

Lipstick and make-up   Dry-cleaning fluid.

Milk   Wash normally on cold cycle.

Mud   For red clay mud, apply dry-cleaning fluid then wash. For black mud, wash in the washing machine.

Nail polish   Apply acetone, not nail polish remover.

Paint For water-based paint, use methylated spirits. For oil-based paints, use turpentine.

Rust Use descaler or lemon juice and salt.

Sap Apply dry-cleaning fluid.

Shoe polish Use methylated spirits.

Soft drinks Treat as though it's a fruit stain because soft drinks are made of vegetable dyes.

Sweat Make a paste of *Vanish Oxi Action* and water and leave on the stain for 15 minutes before washing normally.

Tar Use baby oil, kerosene or dry-cleaning fluid.

Urine Wash in washing powder and dry in sunshine.

Vomit Washing powder, sunshine or *Vanish*, washing machine and dryer.

Wax Ice, dry-cleaning fluid, talcum powder.

Wine New red wine – vinegar.
Old red wine – glycerine, bicarb and detergent.
White wine – vinegar.

❏ To soften towels, mix 30g of bicarb with the washing powder and add 60 ml of vinegar to the rinse water. For really dirty towels, soak them overnight in a solution of 480 ml of white vinegar to a bucket of water. Then wash them normally. You'll find that they're much softer and the fibres won't be prickly any more.

❏ If you want to anti-static your underwear, petticoats, bras and nylon knits, add a small quantity of hair conditioner to the rinse water when you're washing them.

❏ When washing silk, add 1 teaspoon of salt or vinegar to the rinse water. This will help keep the silk soft and prevent the colour from running.

CLEANING THE WASHING MACHINE

Q: 'My washing machine is 20 years old,' reports Wendy. 'It's still working remarkably well, but has a mildewy smell. Is there a solution?'

Problem:	**Mildew smell in washing machine.**
What to use:	**New hose; or bicarb, vinegar.**
How to apply:	The smell could be from a variety of sources. Check the netting sections in the lint catchers first. The smell could also come from the hose, which is very easy to change. Another source could be the joints in the plumbing. If it's from the machine bowl, when it's dry, wipe it with bicarb and vinegar. If the smell persists, run the washing machine on empty with 115 g of bicarb and add 480 ml of vinegar during the rinse cycle.

Q: 'I've got black stuff in my washing machine,' says Ngaire. 'What should I do?'

Problem:	**Black stuff in washing machine.**
What to use:	**Bicarb, vinegar; or replace seals.**
How to apply:	Add 60 g of bicarb to hot washing water. Then add 120 ml of vinegar to the rinse water. If this doesn't work, replace the seals on your washing machine.

HAND WASHING

Hand wash in a sink or a bucket. You can also use the hand wash setting on the washing machine, though I prefer not to. Only ever wash delicates or wool in blood-heat water. To test for blood heat, sprinkle a few drops of water on the inside of your wrist. If you can't feel the water – that is, if it's the same temperature as your wrist – it's blood heat.

HANGING OUT THE WASHING

If I hang something on the washing line contrary to my mother's technique, and she visits, she re-pegs it! One friend was taught to hang her washing with towels on the outside and underwear on the inside so people wouldn't be exposed to her delicates! These days, we're more likely to put clothes in the dryer but it means missing out on one of the best antibacterial cleaners around – the sun. The sun also adds fragrance to your clothes so I suggest making the effort to hang your clothes on the line. The first rule of hanging out the washing is everyone hates ironing – so hang it flat!

When you hang out your washing, hang each item by the strongest section of the garment and always place pegs in unobtrusive spots.

Trousers and skirts should be hung from the waistband. Shirts should be hung from the tails and pegged on the side seams. Shirts can also be put on a coathanger with a plastic shopping bag over the wire to prevent rusting.

Woollens are best dried lying flat on a white towel. If you have to hang something woollen, put an old stocking through the sleeves and peg the stocking to the line.

Use plastic bags to hang delicates on the clothesline. Place the plastic bag over the line and drape the delicates over the bag, then wrap the bag back over the delicates and peg.

Never hang silk on a windy day because the fibres tangle and are difficult to smooth out.

You're less like to get holes if you hang socks by the tops rather than the toes. Hang anything with a nap or fluff with the fluff surfaces facing each other. This works particularly well with towels that have a velvety finish on one side and a normal finish on the other. Drape the towel in half over the line with the 'velvet' side on the inside. They'll take longer to dry but it's worth it when one side is fluffy and soft.

Old netted bags from the fruit shop make great peg bags because water drains through them. Wrap the netted bag around a coathanger that has been opened into a circle. The hook makes it easy to hang.

To stop birds hovering over your clothesline and potentially soiling your clothes, tie some coloured ribbons to the line and allow them to flutter. You could also hang some old CDs on the line. Birds don't like sharp movements.

TUMBLE DRYING

Drying in the sun is preferable but I know that's not always an option. Before using your dryer make sure you clean the lint catcher. To cut back on ironing, fold your clothes as soon as they come out of the dryer. If you're in a hurry and need to speed up the drying process, put a dry tea towel in with your clothes. It will absorb moisture.

To get rid of static, wash and dry synthetics separately from clothes made of natural fibres. Never overdry synthetic fibres. Remove them from the dryer slightly damp and hang to dry naturally either on a clothesline or on hangers.

IRONING

Many years ago when my eldest daughter was a baby, I used to iron professionally. One of the main rules of good ironing is to go with the grain. Find out which way the grain runs by holding the fabric and pulling it. If it's taut, you're on the grain. If you have stretch, you're not on the grain.

I like to iron clothes while they're slightly damp because it speeds up the process. Have some water in a spray pack and squirt a mist over the clothes before running the iron over them. I also like to set the iron on low temperatures and use lots of steam.

When you're ironing wool, use a damp white linen tea towel over the top. Rest and press the iron but don't leave it in the one spot for too long.

Use spray starches sparingly because they can damage your clothes and make your floors slippery.

I like to protect buttons on shirts by making a cardboard cutout like a thick letter 'c' and placing this under the button. Slide the iron between the shirt and the cardboard. I have my 'c' tied to the iron with a piece of elastic.

To sharpen pleats when ironing, lay the garment over the end of the ironing board and, using glass-headed or steel-headed pins, pin the pleats into position on the ironing board. Hold the pleat taut at both ends. Put a damp cloth over the pleat and run the iron gently up and down. For sharp, long-lasting creases, rub soap down the inside of the crease before you iron the garment. This will stop your trousers getting baggy knees!

Light scorch marks from an iron can be removed from white linen with a small piece of white cloth that has been soaked in a solution of 3 per cent hydrogen peroxide. Place it over the damaged area then run a hot iron over the top. Make sure you test a small patch first.

The legs of old pyjamas make great ironing-board covers. Secure them with safety pins underneath the board.

Speed up the ironing process by putting a sheet of aluminium foil under the ironing board cover.

Clean an iron when it's cold with bicarb and vinegar. Just make sure you clean it all off properly with water before using it again. To clean the sticky build-up on the bottom of the iron, get a piece of rough blotting paper, preferably white, and rub the hot iron backwards and forwards over it until no more marks come off.

Q: 'Is there any way to unpleat permanent pleating?' asks Alison.

Problem:	**Unpleating permanent pleating.**
What to use:	**Steam from the iron.**
How to apply:	The effectiveness of this technique will depend on whether the fabric is natural or synthetic. For natural fabrics, remove the pleat using lots of steam from the iron. It's very difficult to get pleats out of synthetic fabrics because they have a memory and return to their original pleats.

Q: 'What's the best way to iron a damask tablecloth?' asks Sue.

Problem:	**Ironing damask.**
What to use:	**Old blanket, iron.**
How to apply:	Make sure the ironing board has thick padding. An

old folded blanket will do. Slightly dampen the table-cloth then iron with the warp of the fabric. The warp goes down the fabric; the weft goes across the fabric.

IRONING WITHOUT AN IRON

To stiffen or smooth tulle, nylon and other fabrics you can't iron, put 1 tablespoon of uncoloured pure soap flakes into a spray bottle and mix with 1 litre of water. Shake the mixture until the soap flakes have completely dissolved and then spray the fabric. Pull the fabric straight and dry it with a hairdryer. Don't hold the hairdryer too close or the heat will melt the fabric. The mixture stiffens and irons at the same time.

FOLDING

The general principle for folding is to have as few folds as possible. Size up the space you have available and then work out the least number of folds for the greatest surface area of the shelf or drawer. Never put a fold down the front of a garment.

Fold socks by matching the tops together and folding three edges over your hand and the other edge over itself. Then remove your hand. Another way is to lay the socks flat, fold them at the heels and pull the top edge over your hand. Then remove your hand.

Fold a tea towel in six squares. Fold towels in four or six depending on the size of the shelf. You can also fold towels in half and then roll them up. This helps them to stay fluffy and looks good.

To prevent creasing in good tablecloths, place a piece of acid-free paper along the middle line.

Outside

The garden used to be just a patch of lawn, a shed and a Hills hoist. These days you've got tiles, paving stones, decks, barbecues, fences, feature walls, pool surrounds and the rest of the landscaping to look after. Fortunately, much of it can be weather-proofed and spill-proofed so you can play, entertain and tinker with ease.

DON'T PAINT IN YOUR GOOD CLOTHES: PHIL'S STORY

Incident: 'I was helping a mate paint his fence. But I didn't change my clothes and, wouldn't you know it, I got paint on my shorts. The other complication is I don't know what kind of paint it is. Can I rescue the shorts? I really like them!'

Solution: To work out what kind of paint it is, get three small containers – one each of turpentine, methylated spirits and acetone. Dip a cotton bud in each one and apply it to the stain, then rub the stain between your thumb and forefinger. Whichever takes colour first is the solvent. Then dip two cotton wool balls in the solvent and place them on the top and bottom sides of the paint mark. Wipe the top cotton wool ball in circles until the paint is removed, working from the outside to the inside of the stain. If this doesn't work or if the paint mark is old, soak the painted part of the shorts in the appropriate solvent and then apply the cotton wool balls.

WOODEN DECKING

A friend of mine bought a beautiful house situated on top of an escarpment, with massive wooden decks from which to enjoy the vista. But because the place hadn't been lived in for ten years, lots of birds and animals had taken up residence on the decks and they were badly stained. The solution involved some methylated spirits, tea, and lots of scrubbing. Prevention is always better than the cure!

Whether you should seal wood depends on the wood. Some woods such as teak, oak and treated cedar can handle exposure to the elements. But if you don't want it to wear or change colour, treat it with tung oil or a good outdoor sealant. If you have logs from the 1970s get rid of them because most were treated with copper and arsenic and are toxic. Remove them with great care.

There are some significant differences between cleaning sealed and unsealed wood and if you mix them up, you'll be in trouble. Clean sealed wood with 3 teaspoons of washing-up liquid in a bucket of warm water. Use a broom rather than a mop because it can reach into all the crevices.

Don't use detergent on unsealed wood because it dries it out and causes splinters. Unsealed wood should be cleaned with 1 bucket of warm water and 240 ml of vinegar and a couple of drops of eucalyptus oil. The eucalyptus oil both cleans and feeds the wood. But don't use eucalyptus oil on painted surfaces because it's a paint stripper. Rinse a pot of strong tea (use 4–5 tea bags) in a bucket of hot water and mop the wood. This will help prevent it going that silvery colour.

BRICKS AND TERRACOTTA PAVING STONES

Bricks and pavers can be cleaned with bicarb and vinegar. Sprinkle the bicarb then splash vinegar over the top. Wipe it down with a stiff broom then rinse with water. To deter mould and algae, add a couple of drops of oil of cloves to the rinse water. If you want to encourage mould and mosses, add yoghurt to the rinse water.

Problem:	**Masonry beetle in the mortar.**
What to use:	*WD-40.*
How to apply:	Use the extension nozzle on the *WD-40* and spray into the holes dug by the masonry beetle. This kills them.

Q:

'Is there anything you can do if you've spilled methylated spirits on spray-on faux brick?' asks Amanda. 'It's left white scaly marks between the bricks.'

Problem:	**Methylated spirits on faux brick.**
What to use:	**Surface insecticide spray; or methylated spirits, shellac, cloth.**
How to apply:	The white marks indicate there's shellac or a similar kind of sealant in the faux brick. To get rid of the marks, use surface insecticide spray on them. It contains kerosene and will remove the marks. To seal the faux bricks, mix 1 part methylated spirits to 1 part shellac and apply with a cloth.

GLAZED TILES

Clean tiles with a mild detergent solution. If your tiles have a tendency to become slippery, create a non-skid surface by adding vinegar to the rinse water. Seal terracotta or Spanish quarry tiles with a proprietary product or make your own temporary sealant with 1 part *Unibond PVA* to 20 parts water. Apply with a mop. (Make sure you wash the mop with soap and water afterwards or it will stiffen.) If the tiles are particularly slippery, mop the floor then scatter a small amount of sand over the surface, then mop again. I did exactly this at my doctor's surgery because I was worried someone would slip on the sloping tiled path. It lasts for about three months.

Q: 'I've got some lovely camellia plants and palms in my courtyard,' reports Shirley. 'But the petals and leaves are leaving dark stains on the ceramic tiles. Is there a solution?'

    Problem: **Plant stains on tiles.**
What to use: **Effervescent denture tablet, wet cloth; or bicarb, vinegar, brush, mop.**
How to apply: Place 1 effervescent denture tablet on the stain and then place a wet cloth over the top and leave overnight. Alternatively, sprinkle bicarb and splash vinegar over the area with a brush, scrub and leave for two hours. Then rinse with a mop and water.

Q: 'We've been meaning to seal our terracotta tiles,' says Pat. 'But, of course, I managed to spill some two-stroke fuel on them before we did. Is there anything I can do?'

    Problem: **Fuel on unsealed tiles.**
What to use: **Mask, bucket, chlorine, brush, vinegar.**
How to apply: Put on a mask and in a large bucket of water, mix 10 per cent of the amount of chlorine you would normally use in the pool each day (see the directions on the packet). Then scrub the stain with a brush to remove the oil. Rinse thoroughly. Make sure you still have your mask on when you neutralise the chlorine with a splash of vinegar. Then seal the tile as described above. You can also buy commercial sealers.

STONE AND SANDSTONE

The best way to clean stone and sandstone is with the pool-cleaning product *Surex Oxysure*. *Surex* is an alternative to chlorine and doesn't kill plants like chlorine does. Use 1 cap of *Surex* per bucket of water and apply with a broom. Leave it for a couple of hours then rinse with water. Add a couple of drops of oil of cloves to the rinse water to inhibit mould, or add yoghurt to encourage mould and mosses.

Problem: **Paint splashes on sandstone.**

What to use: **Methylated spirits, stiff brush; or turpentine, stiff brush; or methylated spirits, cloth, brush; or cloth, soap.**

How to apply: If the paint is water-based, put methylated spirits on the end of a stiff brush and work out the paint. If the paint is oil-based, use turpentine the same way. If the stain is old, leave a methylated spirits soaked cloth on water-based paint for a while then scrub it with a brush. If the paint is oil-based, soak a cloth in hot water and soap and place it over the paint first.

Q: 'I've got some purple droppings on my sandstone patio,' reports Shelly. 'I think it's from a bird. Can I get rid of them?'

Problem: **Bird droppings on sandstone.**

What to use: **Dry-cleaning fluid, cotton wool ball, damp rag.**

How to apply: In most cases, bird droppings will fade in sunlight over time. The purple comes from berry juice and can be removed with dry-cleaning fluid. Dab it on with a cotton wool ball. Then rinse with a damp rag.

Q: 'We moved our barbecue recently,' says Robin, 'but some of the fat from the drip tray fell onto our coloured sandstone patio. How can we get it off?'

Problem:	Oil/fat on sandstone pavers.
What to use:	Mask, swimming pool chlorine, scrubbing brush, vinegar.
How to apply:	The fumes are very strong so wear a mask. Mix $^1/_4$ tablet of swimming pool chlorine in a bucket of water. Apply this mixture to the stain and scrub with a brush. Neutralise with vinegar, then rinse with water.

CONCRETE

Concrete is best cleaned with bicarb and vinegar. Sprinkle the bicarb over the surface, splash the vinegar on top and scrub with a broom. Then rinse with water. Hydrochloric, or muriatic, acid is often suggested to clean concrete. I don't recommend this because it's toxic, difficult to use and can cause corrosion in bricks. To stop leaves staining the concrete and to make grease removal easier, seal concrete with a proprietary product or with a temporary sealant of 1 part *Unibond PVA* to 20 parts water. Apply with a mop. Make sure you rinse your mop afterwards or it will stiffen.

Problem:	Ivy suckers stuck on concrete/brick.
What to use:	Heat gun, stiff brush.
How to apply:	Apply a heat gun to the suckers until they go hard. Allow them to cool and dry, then scrub them off with a stiff brush.

Doormats

I always have a mat at the front and back doors of the house. It's also a good idea to have mats on the inside to prevent dirt tracking into the house. If you don't want to use a mat inside, spray the carpet regularly with Scotchguard. It's also handy to have a shoe cupboard near the back door for dirty wellies. Alternatively, go old-fashioned and use a boot scraper.

OUTDOOR FURNITURE

Outdoor furniture can be made of sealed or unsealed wood, aluminium, glass, plastic, cane or polycarbonate.

To clean sealed wood, use a mild detergent solution. Many outdoor settings are made of red cedar, which can be cleaned with water. Re-stain it every three years. Painted surfaces should be cleaned in a mild detergent solution.

To clean unsealed wood, add 240 ml of vinegar and a couple of drops of eucalyptus oil to a bucket of water and wipe with a cloth.

To clean aluminium settings, use bicarb and vinegar. You could also try cold black tea! I discovered this recently when I accidentally spilled some tea over aluminium meshing and it came up like glass! Have one sponge with bicarb on it and another soaked in vinegar. Press the vinegar sponge through the bicarb sponge and wipe. You can remove water marks the same way.

To clean polycarbonate or plastic, use a mild detergent solution. Don't confuse polycarbonate with polyacetate. Polyacetate or polyurethane can be cleaned with *Brasso* but this cleaning method ruins polycarbonate. Don't risk it if you're not sure. If you have scratches, use whiting and glycerine. Mix them to the consistency of runny cream, then rub over the scratches with a silk cloth. It's best not to leave opaque polycarbonate in the sun because it becomes weak and a chair may collapse while you're sitting in it – as happened to me at a party one time. I looked like a turtle with my arms flailing around! It was embarrassing, but very funny.

To clean cane and wicker, scrub with soap and water, leave in the sun to dry and seal with shellac or a good outdoor sealant. Spray the sealant on if possible with a plastic spray bottle. Clean the spray bottle with methylated spirits afterwards.

Some outdoor chairs are made of shade cloth and should be washed regularly with mild soapy water. Wash them after it rains because they collect mildew. Add a couple of drops of oil of cloves to the rinse water.

Where possible, keep outdoor cushions under cover when you're not using them. A potential hazard with outdoor furniture is the nasty surprises that take up residence under the table. Keep spiders away by regularly wiping some lemon oil on the underside of it.

Problem:	**Outdoor furniture has gone grey in the sun.**
What to use:	**Strong solution of tea, varnish.**
How to apply:	Wash it with a strong solution of tea before re-varnishing it.

Problem:	**Rust on cast iron.**
What to use:	**Vinegar, wire brush, rust converter.**
How to apply:	Loosen the rust with vinegar then scrub with a wire brush. Then apply rust converter. This produces a hard surface that you can then repaint.

UMBRELLAS, AWNINGS AND SHADE CLOTH

These are essential in a hot summer. Clean canvas with 450 g of salt added to a small bucket of water and apply with a brush or broom. Leave to dry then rinse the salt away.

Clean plastic with water. If it's very dirty, add some detergent to the water.

Raffia umbrellas attract bugs so hose or wash them regularly and spray with surface insecticide.

Metal poles can be cleaned with graphite. Rust can be cleaned with glycerine.

Plastic attachments should be cleaned with glycerine.

Problem:	**Mildew on canvas.**
What to use:	**Strong salt solution, bucket, brush or broom, oil of cloves, spray bottle.**
How to apply:	Scrub the canvas with 450 g of salt added to a small bucket of water and apply with a brush or broom. Leave it to dry. There should be a lot of salt on the surface. Scrub it again to help loosen any remaining mildew. Hose or wash it clean in a sunny spot. Then spray the canvas with a few drops of oil of cloves and water in a spray pack. This will prevent the mildew returning.

Caring for rubber

Never leave anything made of rubber sitting in the sunshine. This includes flippers, masks, trays or seats. To prevent rubber perishing, rub it with talcum powder after cleaning. If it has perished, rub some salt on the perished area then dust with talcum powder. The salt acts as a sander.

BARBECUES

Barbecue hotplates are made of cast iron and should be cleaned after each use. It's preferable to do this while the barbecue is still warm. Pour a little oil over it then wipe with a newspaper. Sprinkle some bicarb and splash over some vinegar. Then scrub with a paper towel. Give the hotplate a light oiling once it's cooled, to prevent rusting. If the stains are really stubborn, try bicarb and vinegar then apply sugar and vinegar to a hot hotplate. Keep the heat on until the vinegar completely evaporates. Then oil the barbecue. Turn it off and wipe down with a towel. The reason sugar helps is that it bonds with the dirt and burns. The oil goes under the sugar and lifts it off. This is how they clean hotplates at McDonald's!

To stop the oils in fish staining the barbecue and leaving a smell, place a piece of aluminium foil on the hotplate and cook the fish on top of it. Wrap aluminium foil around the fish to steam it.

THE GARDEN

I love spending time in the garden. And I'm particular about avoiding toxins. My preference is for natural rather than chemical solutions. For example:

To keep birds away, hang old CDs in the trees.

To grow moss in the garden put a handful of moss into a bowl with 1 teaspoon of sugar and 1 can of beer and mix with a hand-cranked cake beater until all the ingredients resemble a chunky soup. Spread the mixture over rocks or any ground where you want moss to grow and don't water it for at least 24 hours. Then water it very lightly, making sure you don't wash the moss away. To encourage algae and lichen, paint everything with yoghurt.

Problem:	**Aphids.**
What to use:	**Detergent, cooking oil, water, spray bottle.**
How to apply:	Thoroughly mix 1 tablespoon of detergent and 240 ml of cooking oil. Add 2–3 teaspoons of this mixture to 240 ml of water, put it into a spray bottle and spray your plants.

Problem:	**Snails and slugs getting into pot plants.**
What to use:	*Vaseline*.
How to apply:	Rub some *Vaseline* each month on the outside of pot plants.

Problem:	**Preventing mildew forming on terracotta pots.**
What to use:	***Unibond PVA*, water, oil of cloves.**
How to apply:	To stop mildew forming on terracotta pots, seal with a mixture of 1 part *Unibond PVA*, 3 parts water and a couple of drops of oil of cloves. It should be the consistency of runny cream. Paint it over the pots and let them dry inside and out.

Snail-proofing your vegetable patch

If slugs and snails are eating your vegetable patch, crush a whole clove of garlic and steep it in 1 litre of water for a couple of hours. Strain it, then spray the liquid on your vegetables. Another way to stop them is to put a circle of sand or sawdust around each vegetable. Snails and slugs don't like either so they won't cross them to eat the vegetables. To make a trap for snails, cut an orange in half, eat the flesh and half-fill the two orange skins with beer. Put these near the veggie patch and the snails will climb in and won't be able to get out. You could also persuade children to collect them in return for pocket money.

Garden ponds

If you have a garden pond, stick water hyacinths in it. They clean the water, are easily pulled out with a rake and make a great fertiliser.

Statues

Statues can be large or small. If you want to encourage moss to grow on them, paint them with a mixture of skimmed milk and yoghurt. If you can, use a yoghurt containing acidophilus. To inhibit moss and mould, paint with 1 part oil of cloves to 50 parts water.

Gardening tools

Leaf blowers are the jet-skis of the land – the latest gadgets to wake up the country on a Sunday morning. Along with the lawnmower, strimmer and other equipment, they should be stored in a cool, dark place. Protect all blades against rust by wiping them with machine oil applied with a cloth. Wipe the outside of the lawnmower, strimmer, etc, with a mild detergent solution.

Don't throw old hedge clippers away. Pull them apart and recycle them into trowels, a hole digger or to cut grass edges around concrete.

SWIMMING POOL

If it's hot and you've got a pool, everyone wants to be your friend. But despite the range of accessories, cleaning a pool can be painstaking. If it's all a bit too much for you, hire a professional pool cleaner.

There are a few things that need regular maintenance. Firstly, make sure the water level is high enough. Maintaining the right pH level is also very important. You should already have a testing kit but if you don't, you can buy them. Be aware that chlorine is affected by the sun. The more sunny days there are, the more chlorine you'll need to use. If you don't like chlorine, try *Surex Oxysure*.

Skim the top of the pool regularly to collect leaves so they don't clog the filter. In fact, don't leave anything in the pool because it could get caught in the filter.

Clean the tiles with *Gumption* and a stiff brush. Create traction on slate surrounds by mixing 1 part *Surex Oxysure*, 20 parts water and 225 g of sand. Clear potentially slippery moss from stones with chlorine.

Make sure the pool is fenced and has a childproof lock. Keep the lock oiled because chlorine can cause corrosion. It's a good idea to have a sign illustrating how to perform CPR in case of an emergency.

Keep sunscreen and spare towels near the pool. That way you won't have wet feet tramping through the house.

Q: 'My swimming pool has a stain all around the wall edge,' reports John. 'The wall's made of pebble-crete.'

Problem:	**Stain around swimming pool.**
What to use:	**Stiff brush, *Gumption*.**
How to apply:	It's painstaking but it works. Get a stiff brush, put some *Gumption* on it and scrub the stain off bit by bit.

SPAS AND SAUNAS

Bacteria can thrive in spas. Backflush with vinegar after every second use and change the water regularly. Maintain the right chemical level, which is generally higher than that for swimming pools. Check the manufacturer's instructions. If the spa has a wooden surround, add a couple of drops of oil of cloves to the rinse water to keep mildew at bay.

Maintain the heating and filter units of a sauna by cleaning regularly according to the manufacturer's instructions. Add a few drops of oil of cloves to keep mildew away and add your favourite herbs to the hot stones for a super sauna.

PETS

Pet baskets and kennels should be elevated so air can circulate. Put some bricks underneath or build some stilts. Hand wash all pet bedding regularly, adding a couple of drops of oil of pennyroyal to the water to prevent fleas. **Don't do this if you or your pet is pregnant.** Oil of pennyroyal kills existing fleas and deters new ones. You can apply it by rubbing your hands with it then rubbing the coat of the dog or cat. You can also add a few drops to the pet's bath. Spray the inside of kennels and baskets with a mixture of 1 teaspoon of oil of pennyroyal to 1 litre of water in a spray bottle. **Again, this shouldn't be used by pregnant women or pregnant pets.**

To prevent cats coming into the yard, spread *Vicks Vaporub* onto a few stones. Turn them over to prevent sun and rain damage.

To stop dogs digging in a particular area, bury some of their poo in the spot and they'll stay away. To encourage digging, leave bones in a particular spot.

How to wash a cat

Do this regularly if there are people in the house who are allergic to cats. With this cleaning technique, you won't be left with scratch marks across your face! Secure a tea towel over the cat's head and front legs, wrapping it firmly. It won't be able to scratch and the darkness calms it. Clean the back with a pet brush. Then wrap the tea towel over the cat's back legs and wipe the front with a washer going from front to back. Don't use a brush because it irritates them. Use a pet shampoo over the entire cat and don't forget to add a couple of drops of oil of pennyroyal to deter fleas **(but do not use if you or your pet is pregnant).** Pamper the cat afterwards so it has a positive association with washing.

DUSTBIN AREA

When I was at primary school, we had a goat that ate the rubbish!
With contemporary bins, deter flies and dogs by adding a couple of
drops of lavender oil to a paper towel and wiping it around the edge
of the bin. To keep fleas and mites away, wipe some oil of pennyroyal. Lemon oil will keep spiders away. To preserve the
environment, try to avoid using plastic bags. Instead, put rubbish
directly into the bin or wrap it in newspaper.

GARAGE AND DRIVEWAY

Two of the best ways to clean oil stains and other scum off a
driveway or garage floor is to scrub with bicarb and vinegar or spray
it with diluted chlorine. Leave it until almost dry, then give it a good
sweep with a nylon broom before hosing or washing it down. If you
have plants nearby, substitute *Surex Oxysure* for the chlorine. You
can also clean oil stains with the carbonated drink *Coca-Cola*. If you
do, wash the area well or ants will be attracted to it.

CARS

Clean upholstery and carpet in the car as you would the same
fabrics in the house. To add another layer of protection, spray
Scotchguard each time you vacuum. Clean plastics with glycerine on
a cloth and keep an old pair of pantyhose in the glovebox to clean
windows. To protect the heel of your shoe when you're driving,
either fix a piece of towel to the mat, or have a dedicated pair of
driving shoes.

Problem: Scratches in the dashboard or on plastic surfaces.
What to use: Glycerine, cloth.
How to apply: Add 1 part glycerine to 5 parts warm water then wipe over the surface with a cloth. Glycerine will also give the surface a good sheen.

Problem: Sticky adhesive on car window.
What to use: Cling film, detergent.
How to apply: Tear off a piece of cling film larger than the size of the adhesive. Mix 1 part detergent and 20 parts water and spray on the cling film then place this over the sticker. Leave it for about five minutes or until the adhesive comes loose. Then peel off the cling wrap. The adhesive will peel off, too.

Q: 'I've got the smell of mould in my car,' says Pete. 'I think the carpet must have got wet at some stage. What do you suggest?'

Problem: Mould smell in car.
What to use: Oil of cloves.
How to apply: The smell comes from the bacteria and mould and the best way to fix it is with sunshine. If possible, take the carpet out of the car and leave it in the sun. If you can't, park the car on a funny angle or slope and leave the doors open so sun gets in. Or wipe the carpet with a little oil of cloves.

CARAVANS AND BOATS

Some caravans and boats could be considered houses in their own right. I won't include a comprehensive guide to their upkeep but here are a couple of real-life problems.

Q: 'I've got a pop-top caravan and the nylon zips have become stuck,' says Rick.

Problem:	**Sticky nylon zips.**
What to use:	**Glycerine; or lead pencil or graphite.**
How to apply:	Wipe the zipper with glycerine. For metal zips, use a lead pencil or graphite.

Q: Val's husband and son are going away for a boys' holiday in their caravan. But they've left her with the job of fixing the scratches on the polycarbonate dome skylight. 'We were advised to clean them with a particular product, but it scratched them. Are there any solutions?'

Problem:	**Scratches in polycarbonate.**
What to use:	**Whiting, glycerine, silk cloth or *Ceramicoat*.**
How to apply:	It's very difficult to take scratches out. One option is to mix whiting and glycerine to a thin consistency, then rub it over the scratches with a silk cloth. The deep marks will be there permanently. Another option is to reglaze the surface. Try a product called *Ceramicoat*. Do a test patch first, and if it works, reglaze the dome in very thin coats. Spray one coat, leave it for 5 minutes, spray another coat and then

leave for 24 hours. Repeat if necessary. To prevent
scratching, use car wax but make sure it doesn't
have a cutting compound.

Q: 'We've got a boat and the inside is covered with
a white nylon carpet,' says Lynn, 'but it's starting to
stain black and mildewy. What can we do? It's
really hard to put new carpet in a boat!'

Problem:	**Mildew in boat carpet.**
What to use:	**Pool chlorine, bucket, water.**
How to apply:	Because the carpet is nylon, wash it with diluted pool chlorine. Use $1/4$ of a tablet of chlorine to a bucket of water.

Index